COMPENDIUM OF THE CONFEDERATE ARMIES

TEXAS

COMPENDIUM OF THE CONFEDERATE ARMIES

TEXAS

Stewart Sifakis

Facts On File®

AN INFOBASE HOLDINGS COMPANY

COMPENDIUM OF THE CONFEDERATE ARMIES: TEXAS

Copyright © 1995 by Stewart Sifakis

Facts On File, Inc.
460 Park Avenue South
New York NY 10016

Library of Congress Cataloging-in-Publication Data

Sifakis, Stewart.
    Compendium of the Confederate armies.

    Includes bibliographical references and indexes.
Contents: Alabama—Florida and Arkansas—North Carolina—
Tennessee—Virginia—Kentucky, Maryland, Missouri and the
Indian units—South Carolina and Georgia—Louisiana—
Mississippi—Texas—Tables of organizations.
ISBN 0- 8160-2293-3
1. Confederate States of America. Army—History.
2. United States—History—Civil War, 1851–1865—
Regimental histories. I. Title.
E546.S58   1992   973.7'42   90–23631

Facts On File books are available at special discounts when purchased in bulk quantities for businesses, associations, institutions or sales promotions. Please call our Special Sales Department in New York at 212/683-2244 or 800/322-8755.

Text design by Ron Monteleone
Printed in the United States of America

MP FOF 10 9 8 7 6 5 4 3 2 1
This book is printed on acid-free paper.

To
the Memory of James Sifakis
1893–1961

CONTENTS

ACKNOWLEDGMENTS

I am deeply indebted for this work to the personnel, past and present, of Facts On File, especially to Edward Knappman, Gerry Helferich, and my editors: Kate Kelly, Helen Flynn, Eleanora von Dehsen, Traci Cothran, Nicholas Bakalar, Susan Schwartz and Michelle Fellner. Thanks also go to Joe Reilly, Michael Laraque, Jackie Massa and Kevin Rawlings. Also I would like to thank the staffs of the National Archives, Library of Congress, the various state archives and the New York Public Library for their patience and assistance. Over the past decades the staff of the National Park Service, Edwin C. Bearss, chief historian, have proven very informative on my frequent visits to the various battlefields. To Shaun and Christina Potter and Sally Gadsby I am indebted for keeping me at my work. For the logistical support of the management of the Hotel Post, Zermatt (Karl Ivarsson, Ursula Waeny and Lesley Dawkins), I am very grateful. And last, but certainly not least, I owe thanks to John Warren for his knowledge of computers, without which this project would have ground to a halt, and to his computer widow, Evelyne.

INTRODUCTION

This work is intended to be the companion set to Frederick H. Dyer's *Compendium of the War of the Rebellion* for the Confederacy. The compendium was first published as a three-volume work in 1909. A study of all the Union regiments, battalions, batteries and independent companies, it has since been reprinted in two- and one-volume editions.

It has been estimated that for every day since the end of the American Civil War, one book, magazine or newspaper article has appeared dealing with some aspect of that fratricidal struggle. Many ask: If so much has been written on the Civil War, is there really a need for more? The answer is an emphatic yes. Many aspects of the conflict have been covered only superficially and require much more in-depth research. But for such research a bedrock of reference works is essential.

There are many such works available, including the U.S. War Department's 128-volume *The War of the Rebellion: A Compilation of the Official Records of the Union and Confederate Armies* and the U.S. Navy Department's 31-volume *Official Records of the Union and Confederate Navies in the War of the Rebellion.* Registers of military personnel include: George W. Cullum's two-volume *Biographical Register of the Officers and Graduates of the United States Military Academy*, Francis B. Heitman's two-volume *Historical Register and Dictionary of the United States Army From Its Organization, September 29, 1789, to March 2, 1903*, Guy V. Henry's two-volume *Military Record of Civilian Appointments in the United States Army*, Robert K. Krick's *Lee's Colonels: A Biographical Register of the Field Officers of the Army of Northern Virginia* and Ezra J. Warner's *Generals in Gray: Lives of the Confederate Commanders* and *Generals in Blue: Lives of the Union Commanders*. Politics are covered in Jon L. Wakelyn's *Biographical Dictionary of the Confederacy* and Ezra J. Warner's and W. Buck Yearns' *Biographical Register of the Confederate Congress*. E. B. Long's *The Civil War Day by Day: An Almanac 1861-1865* provides an excellent chronology. Collective biographies include Mark M. Boatner's *The Civil War Dictionary*, Patricia L. Faust's

Historical Times Illustrated Encyclopedia of the Civil War and Stewart Sifakis' *Who Was Who in the Civil War*. Then, of course there is Dyer's compendium.

To date there has not been a comprehensive equivalent to Dyer's work for the South as a whole. Basically work has been done by individual states. North Carolina has an excellent work currently nearing completion. Other commendable works have been done for Tennessee, Virginia and Texas. Works were begun for Georgia and South Carolina but did not proceed far. State government agencies in Florida and Kentucky made some efforts in the early years after the war. However, none of these draws a consolidated picture of the Confederate States Army. That is where the *Compendium of the Confederate Armies* comes in.

This work is organized into volumes by state. One volume includes the border state units—Kentucky, Maryland and Missouri; units organized directly by the Confederate authorities from various state companies; and those units from the Indian nations allied with the Confederacy. The final volume consists of the tables of organization of the various armies and departments throughout the war.

There are chapters in each volume on the artillery, cavalry and infantry. Those units having a numerical designation are listed first, followed by those units using the name of their commander, home region or some other name. Units are then broken down alphabetically by size—for example, battalions, batteries, companies and regiments. If two or more units still have the same sorting features, they are then further broken down alphabetically by any special designation—1st or 2nd Organization, Local Defense Troops, Militia, Provisional Army, Regulars, Reserves, Sharpshooters, State Guard, State Line, State Troops or Volunteers and so on. The company designation for artillery batteries that served within an artillery battalion or regiment is listed at the end of the battalion or regiment designation. If heavy artillery battalions or regiments served together as a unit through most of the war, they are treated as a whole with no breakdown of the companies.

Each entry starts with the unit's name. Any nicknames or other mistaken designations follow. Then comes a summary of its organizational details: its date and location of organization, mustering into service, the number of companies for battalion organizations, armament for artillery batteries, surrenders, paroles, exchanges and disbandment or mustering out. The next paragraph starts with the first commanding officer and continues with an alphabetical listing of the other field-grade officers. (Captains are listed chronologically for artillery batteries.) The next paragraph is the brigade and higher-level command assignments of the unit. This is followed by a listing of the battles and campaigns the unit was engaged in. Note that the unit was not necessarily present on each date that is indicated for multiday actions. The final paragraph is the suggested further reading, if any.

Because records are incomplete, I have dropped the list of casualties of each unit that Dyer includes for the Northern units. But I have added to Dyer's format by including the first commanding officer and the field-grade officers of each unit. Selected bibliographies are included for each volume. Also, as available, unit histories and personal memoirs are listed with some units as suggested further reading.

TEXAS

TEXAS UNITS

Texas seceded from the Union on February 1, 1861. On the same date the Virginia Convention authorized the governor to call into active service as many volunteers as he might deem to be necessary for the defense of the Old Dominion. The call was not formally issued for another three days. On April 24, 1861, Robert E. Lee was commissioned as the commander of the "military and naval forces of Virginia" with the rank of major general in both the Volunteers and the Provisional Army of Virginia.

There were several specialized types of units organized for the army. The Confederate Congress passed an act authorizing the creation of local Defense Troops units on August 21, 1861. However the Confederate Adjutant and Inspector General's Office did not issue its General Orders #86 outlining the regulations for their organization until June 23, 1863. These units were usually organized on the company and battalion level for defense of the areas in which they were raised. They were frequently composed of employees of government arsenals, armories, bureaus, etc. or from men detailed from regular line units for detached service. Toward the end of the war some of these units were organized into regiments. These units were only to be called into active service when the situation in the vicinity required it.

The Confederate Congress created the Reserves on February 17, 1864, when it expanded conscription to include all white males between 17 and 50. Those under 18 and those over 45 were to be organized in the Reserves, troops that did not have to serve beyond the boundaries of the state.

ARTILLERY

1. TEXAS 1ST FIELD ARTILLERY BATTERY

Also Known As: Waul's Legion Artillery Battery

Nickname: Alamo City Guards

Organization: Organized on February 15, 1861. Attached to Waul's Legion on April 20, 1862. Detached from Waul's Legion later in 1862. It was armed with four guns on March 21, 1864. Captured at Henderson's Hill, Louisiana on March 21, 1864. It was armed with four guns on November 19, 1864. Designated as the 1st Field Artillery Battery on November 19, 1864. It was armed with four 3.67" Rifles in May 1865. Surrendered by General E. K. Smith, commanding Trans-Mississippi Department, on May 26, 1865.

First Commander: William Edgar (Captain)

Captain: James M. Ransom

Assignments: Department of Texas (April 1861-February 1862)

Nichols' Brigade, Eastern District, Department of Texas (February-March 1862)

Artillery, McCulloch's Division, District of Arkansas, Trans-Mississippi Department (August-October 1862)

Artillery, District of West Louisiana, Trans-Mississippi Department (November 1863-September 1864)

8th Mounted Artillery Battalion, Unattached, Trans-Mississippi Department (September-November 1864)

Unattached, Trans-Mississippi Department (December 1864-January 1865)

4th (Squires'-Faries') Artillery Battalion, Trans-Mississippi Department (April-May 1865)

Battles: San Lucas Springs (May 9, 1861)

Red River Campaign (March-May 1864)

Henderson's Hill (March 21, 1864)

2. TEXAS 1ST HEAVY ARTILLERY REGIMENT

Organization: Organized by the increase of the 3rd Artillery Battalion to a regiment on April 28, 1862. Surrendered by General E. K. Smith, commanding Trans-Mississippi Department, on May 26, 1865.

First Commander: Joseph J. Cook (Colonel)

Field Officers: Edward Von Harten (Major)

John H. Manly (Lieutenant Colonel)

3. TEXAS 1ST HEAVY ARTILLERY REGIMENT, 1ST COMPANY A

Nickname: Dixie Grays

Organization: Organized by the assignment of Company A, 3rd Artillery Battalion on April 28, 1862. Became Company A, 7th Artillery Battalion in June 1863.

First Commander: Sidney T. Fontaine (Captain)

Captain: O. G. Jones

Assignments: Eastern District of Texas, Department of Texas (April-May 1862)

Eastern District of Texas (May-August 1862)

District of Texas, Trans-Mississippi Department (August-December 1862)

District of Texas, New Mexico, and Arizona, Trans-Mississippi Department (December 1862-January 1863)

Eastern Sub-district, District of Texas, New Mexico, and Arizona, Trans-Mississippi Department (January-June 1863)

Battles: Galveston (October 5, 1862)

Galveston Island (January 1, 1863)

4. TEXAS 1ST HEAVY ARTILLERY REGIMENT, 2ND COMPANY A

Organization: Organized by the change of designation of Company L, 1st Heavy Artillery Regiment on April 30, 1863. Surrendered by General E. K. Smith, commanding Trans-Mississippi Department, on May 26, 1865.

First Commander: N. J. King (Captain)

Assignments: Eastern Sub-district, District of Texas, New Mexico, and Arizona, Trans-Mississippi Department (April-June 1863)

Debray's Brigade, Scurry's Division [or Eastern Sub-district], District of Texas, New Mexico, and Arizona, Trans-Mississippi Department (June-July 1863)

Eastern Sub-district, District of Texas, New Mexico, and Arizona, Trans-Mississippi Department (July 1863-September 1864)

5th (Hawes') Texas Infantry Brigade, 2nd Texas (Hébert's) Division, 3rd Corps, Trans-Mississippi Department (September 1864-May 1865)

5. TEXAS 1ST HEAVY ARTILLERY REGIMENT, COMPANY B

Organization: Organized by the assignment of Company B, 3rd Artillery Battalion on April 28, 1862. Surrendered by General E. K. Smith, commanding Trans-Mississippi Department, on May 26, 1865.

First Commander: A. R. Wier (Captain)

Captain: J. V. Riley

Assignments: Eastern District, Department of Texas (April-May 1862)

Eastern District of Texas, Trans-Mississippi Department (May-August 1862)

District of Texas, Trans-Mississippi Department (August-December 1862)

District of Texas, New Mexico, and Arizona, Trans-Mississippi Department (December 1862-January 1863)

Eastern Sub-district, District of Texas, New Mexico, and Arizona, Trans-Mississippi Department (January-June 1863)

Debray's Brigade, Scurry's Division [or Eastern Sub-district], District of Texas, New Mexico, and Arizona, Trans-Mississippi Department (June-July 1863)

Eastern Sub-district, District of Texas, New Mexico, and Arizona, Trans-Mississippi Department (July 1863-September 1864)

5th (Hawes') Texas Infantry Brigade, 2nd Texas (Hébert's) Division, 3rd Corps, Trans-Mississippi Department (September 1864-May 1865)

Battles: Galveston (October 5, 1862)

Galveston Island (January 1, 1863)

6. TEXAS 1ST HEAVY ARTILLERY REGIMENT, COMPANY B

See: TEXAS TEEL'S-BENNETT'S ARTILLERY BATTERY

7. TEXAS 1ST HEAVY ARTILLERY REGIMENT, COMPANY C

Organization: Organized by the assignment of Company C, 3rd Artillery Battalion on April 28, 1862. Surrendered by General E. K. Smith, commanding Trans-Mississippi Department, on May 26, 1865.

First Commander: E. B. H. Schneider (Captain)

Captains: Charles T. Willrich

Peter H. Erhard

Assignments: Eastern District, Department of Texas (April-May 1862)

Eastern District of Texas, Trans-Mississippi Department (May-August 1862)

District of Texas, Trans-Mississippi Department (August-December 1862)

District of Texas, New Mexico, and Arizona, Trans-Mississippi Department (December 1862-January 1863)

Eastern Sub-district, District of Texas, New Mexico, and Arizona, Trans-Mississippi Department (January-June 1863)

Debray's Brigade, Scurry's Division [or Eastern Sub-district], District of Texas, New Mexico, and Arizona, Trans-Mississippi Department (June-July 1863)

Eastern Sub-district, District of Texas, New Mexico, and Arizona, Trans-Mississippi Department (July 1863-September 1864)
5th (Hawes') Texas Infantry Brigade, 2nd Texas (Hébert's) Division, 3rd Corps, Trans-Mississippi Department (September 1864-May 1865)
Battles: Galveston (October 5, 1862)
Galveston Island (January 1, 1863)

8.   TEXAS 1ST HEAVY ARTILLERY REGIMENT, COMPANY D

Organization: Organized by the assignment of Company D, 3rd Artillery Battalion on April 28, 1862. Detached as Nichols' Artillery Battery in 1864.
First Commander: Charles M. Mason (Captain)
Captain: William H. Nichols
Assignments: Eastern District, Department of Texas (April-May 1862)
Eastern District of Texas, Trans-Mississippi Department (May-August 1862)
District of Texas, Trans-Mississippi Department (August-December 1862)
District of Texas, New Mexico, and Arizona, Trans-Mississippi Department (December 1862-January 1863)
Eastern Sub-district, District of Texas, New Mexico, and Arizona, Trans-Mississippi Department (January-June 1863)
Debray's Brigade, Scurry's Division [or Eastern Sub-district], District of Texas, New Mexico, and Arizona, Trans-Mississippi Department (June-July 1863)
Eastern Sub-district, District of Texas, New Mexico, and Arizona, Trans-Mississippi Department (July-December 1863)
Battles: Galveston (October 5, 1862)
Galveston Island (January 1, 1863)

9.   TEXAS 1ST HEAVY ARTILLERY REGIMENT, COMPANY E

Organization: Organized by the assignment of Company E, 3rd Artillery Battalion on April 28, 1862. Detached and designated as the 2nd Field Battery on November 19, 1864.
First Commander: Jordan W. Bennett (Captain)
Captain: M. V. McMahan
Assignments: Eastern District, Department of Texas (April-May 1862)
Eastern District of Texas, Trans-Mississippi Department (May-August 1862)
District of Texas, Trans-Mississippi Department (August-December 1862)
District of Texas, New Mexico, and Arizona, Trans-Mississippi Department (December 1862-January 1863)
Eastern Sub-district, District of Texas, New Mexico, and Arizona, Trans-Mississippi Department (January-June 1863)
Debray's Brigade, Scurry's Division [or Eastern Sub-district], District of Texas, New Mexico, and Arizona, Trans-Mississippi Department (June-July 1863)

Eastern Sub-district, District of Texas, New Mexico, and Arizona, Trans-Mississippi Department (July 1863-September 1864)

5th (Hawes') Texas Infantry Brigade, 2nd Texas (Hébert's) Division, 3rd Corps, Trans-Mississippi Department (September 1864-May 1865)

Battles: Galveston (October 5, 1862)

Galveston Island (January 1, 1863)

10. TEXAS 1ST HEAVY ARTILLERY REGIMENT, COMPANY F

Nickname: Davis Guards

Organization: Organized by the assignment of Company F, 3rd Artillery Battalion on April 28, 1862. Surrendered by General E. K. Smith, commanding Trans-Mississippi Department, on May 26, 1865.

First Commander: Frederick Odlum (Captain)

Assignments: Eastern District, Department of Texas (April-May 1862)

Eastern District of Texas, Trans-Mississippi Department (May-August 1862)

District of Texas, Trans-Mississippi Department (August-December 1862)

District of Texas, New Mexico, and Arizona, Trans-Mississippi Department (December 1862-January 1863)

Eastern Sub-district, District of Texas, New Mexico, and Arizona, Trans-Mississippi Department (January-June 1863)

Debray's Brigade, Scurry's Division [or Eastern Sub-district], District of Texas, New Mexico, and Arizona, Trans-Mississippi Department (June-July 1863)

Eastern Sub-district, District of Texas, New Mexico, and Arizona, Trans-Mississippi Department (July 1863-September 1864)

5th (Hawes') Texas Infantry Brigade, 2nd Texas (Hébert's) Division, 3rd Corps, Trans-Mississippi Department (September 1864-May 1865)

Battles: Galveston (October 5, 1862)

Galveston Island (January 1, 1863)

Sabine Pass (September 8, 1863)

11. TEXAS 1ST HEAVY ARTILLERY REGIMENT, COMPANY G

Organization: Organized by the assignment of Company G, 3rd Artillery Battalion on April 28, 1862. Surrendered by General E. K. Smith, commanding Trans-Mississippi Department, on May 26, 1865.

First Commander: Alfred Whittaker (Captain)

Assignments: Eastern District, Department of Texas (April-May 1862)

Eastern District of Texas, Trans-Mississippi Department (May-August 1862)

District of Texas, Trans-Mississippi Department (August-December 1862)

District of Texas, New Mexico, and Arizona, Trans-Mississippi Department (December 1862-January 1863)

Eastern Sub-district, District of Texas, New Mexico, and Arizona, Trans-Mississippi Department (January-June 1863)

Debray's Brigade, Scurry's Division [or Eastern Sub-district], District of Texas, New Mexico, and Arizona, Trans-Mississippi Department (June-July 1863)

Eastern Sub-district, District of Texas, New Mexico, and Arizona, Trans-Mississippi Department (July 1863-September 1864)

5th (Hawes') Texas Infantry Brigade, 2nd Texas (Hébert's) Division, 3rd Corps, Trans-Mississippi Department (September 1864-May 1865)

Battles: Galveston (October 5, 1862)

Galveston Island (January 1, 1863)

12. TEXAS 1ST HEAVY ARTILLERY REGIMENT, COMPANY H

Organization: Organized on April 3, 1862. Surrendered by General E. K. Smith, commanding Trans-Mississippi Department, on May 26, 1865.

First Commander: Thomas J. Catching (Captain)

Assignments: Eastern District, Department of Texas (April-May 1862)

Eastern District of Texas, Trans-Mississippi Department (May-August 1862)

District of Texas, Trans-Mississippi Department (August-December 1862)

District of Texas, New Mexico, and Arizona, Trans-Mississippi Department (December 1862-January 1863)

Eastern Sub-district, District of Texas, New Mexico, and Arizona, Trans-Mississippi Department (January-June 1863)

Debray's Brigade, Scurry's Division [or Eastern Sub-district], District of Texas, New Mexico, and Arizona, Trans-Mississippi Department (June-July 1863)

Eastern Sub-district, District of Texas, New Mexico, and Arizona, Trans-Mississippi Department (July 1863-September 1864)

5th (Hawes') Texas Infantry Brigade, 2nd Texas (Hébert's) Division, 3rd Corps, Trans-Mississippi Department (September 1864-May 1865)

Battle: Galveston Island (January 1, 1863)

13. TEXAS 1ST HEAVY ARTILLERY REGIMENT, COMPANY I

Organization: Organized on May 23, 1862. Surrendered by General E. K. Smith, commanding Trans-Mississippi Department, on May 26, 1865.

First Commander: D. M. Jackson (Captain)

Captain: Henry L. Bolton

Assignments: Eastern District, Department of Texas (May 1862)

Eastern District of Texas, Trans-Mississippi Department (May-August 1862)

District of Texas, Trans-Mississippi Department (August-December 1862)

District of Texas, New Mexico, and Arizona, Trans-Mississippi Department (December 1862-January 1863)

Eastern Sub-district, District of Texas, New Mexico, and Arizona, Trans-Mississippi Department (January-June 1863)

Debray's Brigade, Scurry's Division [or Eastern Sub-district], District of Texas, New Mexico, and Arizona, Trans-Mississippi Department (June-July 1863)

Eastern Sub-district, District of Texas, New Mexico, and Arizona, Trans-Mississippi Department (July 1863-September 1864)

5th (Hawes') Texas Infantry Brigade, 2nd Texas (Hébert's) Division, 3rd Corps, Trans-Mississippi Department (September 1864-May 1865)

Battles: Galveston (October 5, 1862)

Galveston Island (January 1, 1863)

14. TEXAS 1ST HEAVY ARTILLERY REGIMENT, COMPANY K

Organization: Organized on May 30, 1862. Surrendered by General E. K. Smith, commanding Trans-Mississippi Department, on May 26, 1865.

First Commander: David G. Adams (Captain)

Assignments: Eastern District of Texas, Trans-Mississippi Department (May-August 1862)

District of Texas, Trans-Mississippi Department (August-December 1862)

District of Texas, New Mexico, and Arizona, Trans-Mississippi Department (December 1862-January 1863)

Eastern Sub-district, District of Texas, New Mexico, and Arizona, Trans-Mississippi Department (January-June 1863)

Debray's Brigade, Scurry's Division [or Eastern Sub-district], District of Texas, New Mexico, and Arizona, Trans-Mississippi Department (June-July 1863)

Eastern Sub-district, District of Texas, New Mexico, and Arizona, Trans-Mississippi Department (July 1863-September 1864)

5th (Hawes') Texas Infantry Brigade, 2nd Texas (Hébert's) Division, 3rd Corps, Trans-Mississippi Department (September 1864-May 1865)

Battles: Galveston (October 5, 1862)

Galveston Island (January 1, 1863)

15. TEXAS 1ST HEAVY ARTILLERY REGIMENT, COMPANY L

Organization: Organized on June 20, 1862. Redesignated as 2nd Company A, 1st Heavy Artillery Regiment on April 30, 1863.

First Commander: N. J. King (Captain)

Assignments: Eastern District of Texas, Trans-Mississippi Department (June-August 1862)

District of Texas, Trans-Mississippi Department (August-December 1862)

District of Texas, New Mexico, and Arizona, Trans-Mississippi Department (December 1862-January 1863)

Eastern Sub-district, District of Texas, New Mexico, and Arizona, Trans-Mississippi Department (January-April 1863)

Battle: Galveston Island (January 1, 1863)

16. TEXAS 2ND FIELD ARTILLERY BATTERY

Organization: Organized by the detachment of Company E, 1st Heavy Artillery Regiment in early 1864. Designated as the 2nd Field Battery on November 19, 1864. It was armed with two 3.67" Rifles and two 12-lb. Howitzers in May 1865. Surrendered by General E. K. Smith, commanding Trans-Mississippi Department, on May 26, 1865.

First Commander: M. V. McMahan (Captain)

Assignments: Eastern Sub-district, District of Texas, New Mexico, and Arizona, Trans-Mississippi Department (January-March 1864)

Light Artillery, District of West Louisiana, Trans-Mississippi Department (March-September 1864)

1st (Semmes') Horse Artillery Battalion, 2nd (Maxey's) Texas Cavalry Division, 1st Corps, Trans-Mississippi Department (September 1864-February 1865)

1st (Semmes') Horse Artillery Battalion, Trans-Mississippi Department (February-May 1865)

Battles: Red River Campaign (March-May 1864)

Mansfield (April 8, 1864)

Pleasant Hill (April 9, 1864)

17. TEXAS 3RD ARTILLERY BATTALION

Organization: Organization begun on June 29, 1861. Increased to a regiment and designated as the 1st Heavy Artillery Regiment on April 28, 1862.

First Commander: Joseph J. Cook (Major, Lieutenant Colonel)

Field Officer: Augustin S. Labuzan (Major)

18. TEXAS 3RD ARTILLERY BATTALION, COMPANY A

Nickname: Dixie Grays

Organization: Organized in Fayette County in June 1861. Became Company A, 1st Heavy Artillery Regiment on April 28, 1862.

First Commander: Joseph J. Cook (Captain)

Captain: Sidney T. Fontaine

Assignments: Department of Texas (June 1861-February 1862)

Eastern Sub-district, Department of Texas (February-April 1862)

19. TEXAS 3RD ARTILLERY BATTALION, COMPANY B

Organization: Organized on December 7, 1861. Became Company B, 1st Heavy Artillery Regiment on April 28, 1862.
First Commander: Augustin S. Labuzan (Captain)
Captain: A. R. Wier
Assignments: Department of Texas (December 1861-February 1862)
Eastern Sub-district, Department of Texas (February-April 1862)

20. TEXAS 3RD ARTILLERY BATTALION, COMPANY C

Organization: Organized on June 29, 1861. Became Company C, 1st Heavy Artillery Regiment on April 28, 1862.
First Commander: E. B. H. Schneider (Captain)
Assignments: Department of Texas (June 1861-February 1862)
Eastern Sub-district, Department of Texas (February-April 1862)

21. TEXAS 3RD ARTILLERY BATTALION, COMPANY D

Organization: Organized on October 3, 1861. Became Company D, 1st Heavy Artillery Regiment on April 28, 1862.
First Commander: Samuel B. Davis (Captain)
Captain: Charles M. Mason
Assignments: Department of Texas (October 1861-February 1862)
Eastern Sub-district, Department of Texas (February-April 1862)

22. TEXAS 3RD ARTILLERY BATTALION, COMPANY E

Organization: Organized on October 4, 1861. Became Company E, 1st Heavy Artillery Regiment on April 28, 1862.
First Commander: Edward Von Harten (Captain)
Assignments: Department of Texas (October 1861-February 1862)
Eastern Sub-district, Department of Texas (February-April 1862)

23. TEXAS 3RD ARTILLERY BATTALION, COMPANY F

Nickname: Davis Guards
Organization: Organized on December 12, 1861. Became Company F, 1st Heavy Artillery Regiment on April 28, 1862.
First Commander: Frederick Odlum (Captain)
Assignments: Department of Texas (December 1861-February 1862)
Eastern Sub-district, Department of Texas (February-April 1862)

24. TEXAS 3RD FIELD ARTILLERY BATTERY

Nickname: Dixie Grays

Organization: Organized by the change of designation of Company A, 7th Artillery Battalion on November 19, 1864. It was armed with one 3.67" Rifle, one 3" Rifle, one 12-lb. Howitzer, and three 6-lb. Smoothbores from November 1864 to May 1865. Surrendered by General E. K. Smith, commanding Trans-Mississippi Department, on May 26, 1865.

First Commander: O. G. Jones (Captain)

Assignments: Light Artillery, Western Sub-district, District of Texas, New Mexico, and Arizona, Trans-Mississippi Department (November-December 1864)

7th (Slaughter's) Texas Cavalry Brigade, 3rd (Drayton's) Texas Cavalry Division, 3rd Corps, Trans-Mississippi Department (December 1864-February 1865)

Western Sub-district, District of Texas, New Mexico, and Arizona, Trans-Mississippi Department (March-April 1865)

Unattached, Trans-Mississippi Department (April-May 1865)

Battle: Palmetto Ranch (May 12-13, 1865)

25.   TEXAS 4TH ARTILLERY BATTALION

Also Known As: Shea's Artillery Battalion

Organization: Organized with two companies on December 10, 1861. Consolidated with the 8th Infantry Battalion and designated as the 8th Infantry Regiment in February 1863.

First Commander: Daniel D. Shea (Captain, Major)

26.   TEXAS 4TH ARTILLERY BATTALION, COMPANY A

Organization: Organized by the assignment of Shea's Artillery Battery on December 10, 1861. Assigned to the 8th Infantry Regiment in February 1863.

First Commander: Daniel D. Shea (Captain)

Captain: John A. Vernon

Assignments: Department of Texas (December 1861-February 1862)

Eastern District of Texas, Department of Texas (February-May 1862)

Eastern District of Texas, Trans-Mississippi Department (May-August 1862)

District of Texas, Trans-Mississippi Department (August-December 1862)

District of Texas, New Mexico, and Arizona, Trans-Mississippi Department (December 1862-January 1863)

Eastern Sub-district, District of Texas, New Mexico, and Arizona, Trans-Mississippi Department (January-February 1863)

Battle: Lavaca (October 31-November 1, 1862)

27. TEXAS 4TH ARTILLERY BATTALION, COMPANY B

Organization: Organized by the assignment of the Indianola Artillery Guards Artillery Battery on December 10, 1861. Assigned to the 8th Infantry Regiment in February 1863.

First Commander: Joseph M. Reuss (Captain)

Assignments: Department of Texas (December 1861-February 1862)

Eastern District of Texas, Department of Texas (February-May 1862)

Eastern District of Texas, Trans-Mississippi Department (May-August 1862)

District of Texas, Trans-Mississippi Department (August-December 1862)

District of Texas, New Mexico, and Arizona, Trans-Mississippi Department (December 1862-January 1863)

Eastern Sub-district, District of Texas, New Mexico, and Arizona, Trans-Mississippi Department (January-February 1863)

Battle: Lavaca (October 31-November 1, 1862)

28. TEXAS 4TH FIELD ARTILLERY BATTERY

Nickname: Van Dorn Light Artillery

Organization: Organized on July 1, 1861. Surrendered at Arkansas Post, Arkansas on January 11, 1863. It was armed with four guns on April 1, 1864. Designated as the 4th Field Artillery Battery on November 19, 1864. It was armed with two 12-lb. Howitzers and two 12-lb. Napoleons in May 1865. Surrendered by General E. K. Smith, commanding Trans-Mississippi Department, on May 26, 1865. The guns were dumped into the Red River.

First Commander: William T. Mechling (Captain)

Captain: Horace Haldeman

Assignments: Department of Texas (July 1861-February 1862)

Eastern District, Department of Texas (February-May 1862)

Eastern District of Texas, Trans-Mississippi Department (May-August 1862)

Light Artillery, District of Arkansas, Trans-Mississippi Department (August-September 1862)

Deshler's Brigade, Churchill's Division, 2nd Corps, Army of the West, Trans-Mississippi Department (December 1862)

Deshler's Brigade, Churchill's Division, District of Arkansas, Trans-Mississippi Department (December 1862-January 1863)

Randal's Brigade, District of West Louisiana, Trans-Mississippi Department (November 1863)

Randal's-Waul's Brigade, Walker's Division, District of West Louisiana, Trans-Mississippi Department (November 1863-April 1864)

Waul's Brigade, Walker's Division, District of Arkansas, Trans-Mississippi Department (April-May 1864)

Waul's Brigade, Walker's Division, District of Arkansas, Trans-Mississippi
  Department (May-September 1864)
4th (Squires'-Faries') Field Artillery Battalion, 1st (Forney's) Texas Division,
  1st Corps, Trans-Mississippi Department (September 1864-May 1865)
Battles: Arkansas Post (January 4-11, 1863)
Red River Campaign (March-May 1864)
Camden Expedition (March-May 1864)
Mansfield (April 8, 1864)
Pleasant Hill (April 9, 1864)

29.   TEXAS 5TH FIELD ARTILLERY BATTERY

Also Known As: Company A, Willke's Artillery Battalion
Organization: Organized in Fayette County on October 12, 1861. Designated
as the 5th Field Battery on November 19, 1864. It was armed with two 12-lb.
Napoleons and two 6-lb. Smoothbores in May 1865. Surrendered by General
E. K. Smith, commanding Trans-Mississippi Department, on May 26, 1865.
First Commander: Edmund Creuzbaur (Captain)
Captain: Charles Welhausen
Assignments: Department of Texas (October 1861-February 1862)
Western District, Department of Texas (February-May 1862)
Western District of Texas, Trans-Mississippi Department (May-August 1862)
District of Texas, Trans-Mississippi Department (August-December 1862)
District of Texas, New Mexico, and Arizona, Trans-Mississippi Department
  (December 1862-January 1863)
Western Sub-district, District of Texas, New Mexico, and Arizona, Trans-Mis-
  sissippi Department (January-June 1863)
1st Brigade, Bee's Division [or Western Sub-district], District of Texas, New
  Mexico, and Arizona, Trans-Mississippi Department (June-August 1863)
Western Sub-district, District of Texas, New Mexico, and Arizona, Trans-Mis-
  sissippi Department (August-November 1863)
Reserve Artillery, Trans-Mississippi Department (December 1863)
Eastern Sub-district, District of Texas, New Mexico, and Arizona, Trans-Mississippi Department (January-September 1864)
6th (Willke's) Mounted Artillery Battalion, 2nd (Hébert's) Texas Division, 3rd
  Corps, Trans-Mississippi Department (September-November 1864)
7th (Fontaine's-Wilson's) Field Artillery Battalion, 2nd (Hébert's) Texas Division,
  3rd Corps, Trans-Mississippi Department (November 1864-May 1865)
Battle: Calcasieu Pass (May 6, 1864)

30.   TEXAS 6TH FIELD ARTILLERY BATTERY

Nickname: Austin Light Artillery

Organization: Organized in June 1861. Mustered in on October 14, 1861. It was armed with two 24-lb. Howitzers and four 12-lb. Napoleons in August 1862. Designated as the 6th Field Battery on November 19, 1864. It was armed with two 24-lb. Howitzers and two 12-lb. Napoleons in May 1865. Surrendered by General E. K. Smith, commanding Trans-Mississippi Department, on May 26, 1865.

First Commander: H. Willke (Captain)

Captains: R. W. Yates

Samuel W. Allen

Assignments: Department of Texas (June 1861-February 1862)

Western District of Texas, Department of Texas (February-May 1862)

Western District of Texas, Trans-Mississippi Department (May-August 1862)

District of Texas, Trans-Mississippi Department (August-December 1862)

District of Texas, New Mexico, and Arizona, Trans-Mississippi Department (December 1862-January 1863)

Western Sub-district, District of Texas, New Mexico, and Arizona, Trans-Mississippi Department (January-October 1863)

Reserve Artillery, Trans-Mississippi Department (December 1863)

Eastern Sub-district, District of Texas, New Mexico, and Arizona, Trans-Mississippi Department (January-September 1864)

6th (Willke's) Mounted Artillery Battalion, 2nd (Hébert's) Texas Division, 3rd Corps, Trans-Mississippi Department (September-November 1864)

7th (Fontaine's-Wilson's) Field Artillery Battalion, 2nd (Hébert's) Texas Division, 3rd Corps, Trans-Mississippi Department (November 1864-May 1865)

31. TEXAS 7TH ARTILLERY BATTALION

Organization: Organized in June 1863. Surrendered by General E. K. Smith, commanding Trans-Mississippi Department, on May 26, 1865.

First Commander: Sidney T. Fontaine (Major)

32. TEXAS 7TH ARTILLERY BATTALION, COMPANY A

Nickname: Dixie Grays

Organization: Organized by the assignment of 1st Company A, 1st Heavy Artillery Regiment in June 1863. Christmas' Artillery Battery was merged into this company in 1864. Designated as the 3rd Texas Field Artillery Battery [*q.v.*] on November 19, 1864.

First Commander: O. G. Jones (Captain)

Assignments: Luckett's Brigade, Scurry's Division [or Eastern Sub-district], District of Texas, New Mexico, and Arizona, Trans-Mississippi Department (June 1863)

Eastern Sub-district, District of Texas, New Mexico, and Arizona, Trans-Mississippi Department (June-November 1863)

Luckett's Brigade, District of Texas, New Mexico, and Arizona, Trans-Mississippi Department (November-December 1863)

Reserve Artillery, District of Texas, New Mexico, and Arizona, Trans-Mississippi Department (December 1863)

Eastern Sub-district, District of Texas, New Mexico, and Arizona, Trans-Mississippi Department (December 1863-January 1864)

Western Sub-district, District of Texas, New Mexico, and Arizona, Trans-Mississippi Department (January-November 1864)

Battle: Brashear City (June 23, 1863)

33.   TEXAS 7TH ARTILLERY BATTALION, COMPANY B

Organization: Organized by the assignment of Moseley's Artillery Battery in June 1863.   Designated as the 7th Field Artillery Battery on November 19, 1864.

First Commander: William G. Moseley (Captain)

Assignments: Eastern Sub-district, District of Texas, New Mexico, and Arizona, Trans-Mississippi Department (June 1863-January 1864)

Buchel's Brigade, Slaughter's Division [or Eastern Sub-district], District of Texas, New Mexico, and Arizona, Trans-Mississippi Department (January-March 1864)

Eastern Sub-district, District of Texas, New Mexico, and Arizona, Trans-Mississippi Department (January-March 1864)

District of West Louisiana, Trans-Mississippi Department (March-September 1864)

1st (Semmes') Horse Artillery Battalion, 2nd (Maxey's) Texas Cavalry Division, 1st Corps, Trans-Mississippi Department (September-November 1864)

Battles: San Luis Pass [destruction of the *Columbia*] (April 5-6, 1862)

Red River Campaign (March-May 1864)

Mansfield (April 8, 1864)

Pleasant Hill (April 9, 1864)

34.   TEXAS 7TH FIELD ARTILLERY BATTERY

Organization: Organized by the change of designation of Company B, 7th Artillery Battalion on November 19, 1864.   Surrendered by General E. K. Smith, commanding Trans-Mississippi Department, on May 26, 1865.

First Commander: William G. Moseley (Captain)

Assignments: 1st (Semmes') Field [Horse] Artillery Battalion, 1st (Forney's) Texas Division, 1st Corps, Trans-Mississippi Department (November 1864-February 1865)

Artillery, Wharton's Cavalry Corps, Trans-Mississippi Department (March-May 1865)

35. TEXAS 8TH FIELD ARTILLERY BATTERY

Organization: Organized in Bexar County in November 1861. It was armed with four guns from December 1863 to May 1864. It was armed with eight guns in June-July 1864. Designated as the 8th Field Artillery Battery on November 19, 1864. It was armed with two 12-lb. Napoleons and two 12-lb. Howitzers in May 1865. Surrendered by General E. K. Smith, commanding Trans-Mississippi Department, on May 26, 1865.

First Commander: R. B. Maclin (Captain)

Captains: P. Fox

A. E. Dege

Assignments: Department of Texas (November 1861-February 1862)

Eastern District, Department of Texas (February-May 1862)

Eastern District of Texas, Trans-Mississippi Department (May-August 1862)

District of Texas, Trans-Mississippi Department (August-December 1862)

District of Texas, New Mexico, and Arizona, Trans-Mississippi Department (December 1862-January 1863)

Eastern Sub-district, District of Texas, New Mexico, and Arizona, Trans-Mississippi Department (January-November 1863)

Rainey's Brigade, District of Texas, New Mexico, and Arizona, Trans-Mississippi Department (November 1863)

Rainey's Brigade, Slaughter's Division [or Eastern Sub-district], District of Texas, New Mexico, and Arizona, Trans-Mississippi Department (December 1863-January 1864)

Eastern Sub-district, District of Texas, New Mexico, and Arizona, Trans-Mississippi Department (January-March 1864)

Willke's Artillery Battalion, Eastern Sub-district, District of Texas, New Mexico, and Arizona, Trans-Mississippi Department (March-April 1864)

1st Sub-district, District of Texas, New Mexico, and Arizona, Trans-Mississippi Department (April-September 1864)

7th (Fontaine's-Wilson's) Field Artillery Battalion, 2nd (Hébert's) Texas Division, 3rd Corps, Trans-Mississippi Department (November 1864-May 1865)

36. TEXAS 9TH FIELD ARTILLERY BATTERY

Nickname: Lamar Artillery

Organization: Organized in Lamar County in June 1861. Mustered into Confederate service at Paris on June 18, 1861. It was armed with four guns in August-September 1864. Designated as the 9th Field Battery on November 19, 1864. It was armed with two 3" Rifles and two 12-lb. Howitzers in May 1865.

Surrendered by General E. K. Smith, commanding Trans-Mississippi Department, on May 26, 1865.

First Commander: James M. Daniel (Captain)

Assignments: Artillery, Nelson's Division, 2nd Corps, Army of the West, Trans-Mississippi Department (September-October 1862)

Artillery, McCulloch's Division, 2nd Corps, Trans-Mississippi Department (December 1862)

Artillery, Green's Cavalry Division, Sub-district of Southwestern Louisiana, District of West Louisiana, Trans-Mississippi Department (October-December 1863)

Artillery, District of West Louisiana, Trans-Mississippi Department (December 1863-April 1864)

Randal's Brigade, Walker's Division, District of Arkansas, Trans-Mississippi Department (April-May 1864)

Randal's Brigade, Walker's Division, District of West Louisiana, Trans-Mississippi Department (May-September 1864)

4th (Squires'-Faries') Field Artillery Battalion, 1st (Forney's) Texas Division, 1st Corps, Trans-Mississippi Department (September 1864-May 1865)

Battles: Bayou Bourbeau [section] (November 3, 1863)

Operations *vs.* US gunboats near Hog Point, Mississippi River [section] (November 18-21, 1863)

Red River Campaign (March-May 1864)

Camden Expedition (March-May 1864)

Mansfield (April 8, 1864)

Pleasant Hill (April 9, 1864)

37.   TEXAS 10TH FIELD ARTILLERY BATTERY

Organization: Organized on March 1, 1861. It was armed with six guns on May 20, 1864. It was armed with four guns on November 19, 1864. Designated as the 10th Field Artillery Battery on November 19, 1864. It had no guns and was serving with the Department's Reserve Artillery, Battalion in May 1865. Surrendered by General E. K. Smith, commanding Trans-Mississippi Department, on May 26, 1865.

First Commander: J. H. Pratt (Captain)

Captain: H. C. Hynson

Assignments: Department of Texas (April 1861-February 1862)

Western Sub-district, Department of Texas (February-May 1862)

Parsons' Cavalry Brigade, 2nd Corps, Army of the Southwest, Trans-Mississippi Department (September-October 1862)

Hawes' Brigade, Churchill's Division, 2nd Corps, Army of the West, Trans-Mississippi Department (December 1862-January 1863)

Artillery, Walker's Cavalry Division, District of Arkansas, Trans-Mississippi Department (May-September 1863)

Unattached Artillery, Marmaduke's Cavalry Division, District of Arkansas, Trans-Mississippi Department (September 1863-August 1864)

Marmaduke's-Clarks'-Greene's Brigade, Marmaduke's Cavalry Division, District of Arkansas, Trans-Mississippi Department (August-September 1864)

2nd (Pratt's) Horse Artillery Battalion, Price's Cavalry Corps, Trans-Mississippi Department (September 1864-May 1865)

Battles: Little Rock Campaign (August-September 1863)

Pine Bluff (October 25. 1863)

Lake Chicot (June 6, 1864)

Price's Missouri Raid (August-December 1864)

Further Reading: Bailey, Anne J., *Between the Enemy and Texas: Parson's Texas Cavalry in the Civil War.*

38. TEXAS 11TH FIELD ARTILLERY BATTERY

Organization: Organized on April 22, 1862. It was armed with four guns on April 18, 1864. Designated as the 11th Field Artillery Battery on November 19, 1864. It was armed with two 12-lb. Howitzers and four 6-lb. Smoothbores in May 1865. Surrendered by General E. K. Smith, commanding Trans-Mississippi Department, on May 26, 1865.

First Commander: Sylvanus Howell (Captain)

Assignments: Western Sub-district, Department of Texas (April-May 1862)

Western District of Texas, Trans-Mississippi Department (May-August 1862)

Cooper's Brigade, District of Arkansas, Trans-Mississippi Department (September 1862)

Cooper's Brigade, First Division, 1st Corps, Trans-Mississippi Department (October 1862-January 1863)

Cooper's Brigade, Steele's Division, District of Arkansas, Trans-Mississippi Department (April-October 1863)

Cooper's Brigade, District of the Indian Territory, Trans-Mississippi Department (October 1863-July 1864)

Gano's Brigade, Cooper's (Indian) Division, District of the Indian Territory, Trans-Mississippi Department (July-September 1864)

7th (Krumbhaar's) Mounted Artillery Battalion, Cooper's (Indian) Cavalry Division, Trans-Mississippi Department (September-November 1864)

6th (Krumbhaar's) Field Artillery Battalion, 2nd (Maxey's) Texas Cavalry Division, 1st Corps, Trans-Mississippi Department (November 1864-May 1865)

Battles: Newtonia (September 30, 1862)

Old Fort Wayne (October 22, 1862)

Poison Spring (April 18, 1864)
Cabin Creek (September 19, 1864)

39.   TEXAS 12TH FIELD ARTILLERY BATTERY

Nickname: Valverde Artillery
Organization: Organized on November 1, 1862 under authority of Brigadier
General H. H. Sibley on April 30, 1862. It was armed with six guns, which had
been captured at Valverde on February 21, 1862. Designated as the 12th Field
Artillery Battery on November 19, 1864. It was armed with two 3" Rifles and
two 12-lb. Howitzers in May 1865. Surrendered by General E. K. Smith,
commanding Trans-Mississippi Department, on May 26, 1865.
First Commander: Joseph D. Sayers (Captain)
Captain: T. D. Nettles
Assignments: District of Texas, Trans-Mississippi Department (November-
    December 1862)
District of Texas, New Mexico, and Arizona, Trans-Mississippi Department
    (December 1862-January 1863)
Artillery, District of West Louisiana, Trans-Mississippi Department (April-July
    1863)
Artillery, Sub-district of Southwestern Louisiana, District of West Louisiana,
    Trans-Mississippi Department (July-December 1863)
Artillery, District of West Louisiana, Trans-Mississippi Department (December
    1863)
Green's Cavalry Brigade, Eastern Sub-district, District of Texas, New Mexico,
    and Arizona, Trans-Mississippi Department (December 1863-March 1864)
Green's-Bagby's Brigade, Green's Cavalry Division, District of West Louisiana,
    Trans-Mississippi Department (March-September 1864)
1st (Semmes') Horse Artillery Battalion, 2nd (Maxey's) Texas Cavalry Divi-
    sion, 1st Corps, Trans-Mississippi Department (September 1864-February
    1865)
Artillery, Wharton's Cavalry Corps, Trans-Mississippi Department (March-
    May 1865)
Battles: Fort Bisland (April 12-13, 1863)
Bayou Bourbeau [section] (November 3, 1863)
Red River Campaign (March-May 1864)

40.   TEXAS 13TH FIELD ARTILLERY BATTERY

Organization: Organized in 1862. Designated as the 13th Field Artillery
Battery on November 19, 1864. It was armed with one 3" Rifle, 12-lb. Howitzer,
and two 6-lb. Smoothbores in May 1865. Surrendered by General E. K. Smith,
commanding Trans-Mississippi Department, on May 26, 1865.

First Commander: George R. Wilson (Captain)

Captains: Thomas Gonzales

Robert J. Hughes

Assignments: Eastern District of Texas, Trans-Mississippi Department (August 1862)

District of Texas, Trans-Mississippi Department (August-December 1862)

District of Texas, New Mexico, and Arizona, Trans-Mississippi Department (December 1862-January 1863)

Eastern Sub-district, District of Texas, New Mexico, and Arizona, Trans-Mississippi Department (January-June 1863)

Green's Brigade, Green's Cavalry Division, District of West Louisiana, Trans-Mississippi Department [section] (July 1863)

Fontaine's Artillery Battalion, Luckett's Brigade, Scurry's Division [or Eastern Sub-district], District of Texas, New Mexico, and Arizona, Trans-Mississippi Department (June-November 1863)

Buchel's Brigade, Eastern Sub-district, District of Texas, New Mexico, and Arizona, Trans-Mississippi Department (November-December 1863)

Reserve Artillery, District of Texas, New Mexico, and Arizona, Trans-Mississippi Department (December 1863)

Eastern Sub-district, District of Texas, New Mexico, and Arizona, Trans-Mississippi Department (December 1863-February 1864)

Hart's Artillery Battalion, Eastern Sub-district, District of Texas, New Mexico, and Arizona, Trans-Mississippi Department (March-April 1864)

Eastern Sub-district, District of Texas, New Mexico, and Arizona, Trans-Mississippi Department (April-September 1864)

Artillery, 3rd (Drayton's) Texas Cavalry Division, 3rd Corps, Trans-Mississippi Department (September-October 1864)

2nd [or Central] Sub-district, District of Texas, New Mexico, and Arizona, Trans-Mississippi Department (October-November 1864)

Wilson's Artillery Battalion, 2nd (Hébert's) Texas Division, 3rd Corps, Trans-Mississippi Department (December 1864-February 1865)

Central Sub-district, District of Texas, New Mexico, and Arizona, Trans-Mississippi Department (February-May 1865)

Battle: Cox's Plantation (July 12-13, 1863)

41. TEXAS 14TH FIELD ARTILLERY BATTERY

Organization: Organized as a horse artillery battery in September 1862. Designated as the 14th Field Artillery Battery on November 19, 1864. It was armed with four 6-lb. Smoothbores in May 1865. Surrendered by General E. K. Smith, commanding Trans-Mississippi Department, on May 26, 1865.

First Commander: E. Abat (Captain)

Captain: George R. Dashiell

Assignments: District of Texas, Trans-Mississippi Department (September-December 1862)

District of Texas, New Mexico, and Arizona, Trans-Mississippi Department (December 1862-January 1863)

Eastern Sub-district, District of Texas, New Mexico, and Arizona, Trans-Mississippi Department (January-June 1863)

Debray's Brigade, Scurry's Division [or Eastern Sub-district], District of Texas, New Mexico, and Arizona, Trans-Mississippi Department (June 1863)

Eastern Sub-district, District of Texas, New Mexico, and Arizona, Trans-Mississippi Department (June-November 1863)

Luckett's Brigade, Eastern Sub-district, District of Texas, New Mexico, and Arizona, Trans-Mississippi Department (November-December 1863)

Eastern Sub-district, District of Texas, New Mexico, and Arizona, Trans-Mississippi Department (December 1863-May 1864)

Northern Sub-district, District of Texas, New Mexico, and Arizona, Trans-Mississippi Department (May-September 1864)

7th (Krumbhaar's) Mounted Artillery Battalion, Cooper's (Indian) Cavalry Division, Trans-Mississippi Department (September-November 1864)

6th (Krumbhaar's) Field Artillery Battalion, 2nd (Maxey's) Texas Cavalry Division, 1st Corps, Trans-Mississippi Department (November 1864-May 1865)

42. TEXAS 15TH FIELD ARTILLERY BATTERY

Organization: Organized by the change of designation of Company D, 1st Heavy Artillery Regiment in late 1863. Designated as the 15th Field Artillery Battery on November 19, 1864. It was armed with one 3" Rifle, one 12-lb. Howitzer, and two 6-lb. Smoothbores in May 1865. Surrendered by General E. K. Smith, commanding Trans-Mississippi Department, on May 26, 1865.

First Commander: William H. Nichols (Captain)

Assignments: Reserve Artillery, District of Texas, New Mexico, and Arizona, Trans-Mississippi Department (December 1863)

Light Artillery, Eastern Sub-district, District of Texas, New Mexico, and Arizona, Trans-Mississippi Department (December 1863-September 1864)

6th (Willke's) Mounted Artillery Battalion, 2nd (Hébert's) Texas Division, 3rd Corps, Trans-Mississippi Department (September-November 1864)

7th (Fontaine's-Wilson's-Dege's) Field Artillery Battalion, 2nd (Hébert's) Texas Division, 3rd Corps, Trans-Mississippi Department (November 1864-May 1865)

43. TEXAS 16TH FIELD ARTILLERY BATTERY

Organization: Organized by the conversion of Company H, 13th Infantry Regiment on February 11, 1863. It was armed with four guns in January 1864. It was designated as the 16th Field Artillery Battery on November 19, 1864. It was armed with two 12-lb. Howitzers in May 1865. Surrendered by General E. K. Smith, commanding Trans-Mississippi Department, on May 26, 1865.

First Commander: William E. Gibson (Captain)

Assignments: Eastern Sub-district, District of Texas, New Mexico, and Arizona, Trans-Mississippi Department (February-December 1863)

Luckett's Brigade, Slaughter's Division [or Eastern Sub-district], District of Texas, New Mexico, and Arizona, Trans-Mississippi Department (December 1863-January 1864)

Eastern Sub-district, District of Texas, New Mexico, and Arizona, Trans-Mississippi Department (January-March 1864)

Artillery, District of West Louisiana, Trans-Mississippi Department (March-September 1864)

4th (Squires') Mounted Artillery Battalion, 1st (Forney's) Texas Division, 1st Corps, Trans-Mississippi Department (September-November 1864)

4th (Squires'-Faries') Field Artillery Battalion, 2nd (Polignac's) Division, 1st Corps, Trans-Mississippi Department (November 1864-May 1865)

Battle: Red River Campaign (March-May 1864)

44. TEXAS 17TH FIELD ARTILLERY BATTERY

Nickname: Texas Guards

Organization: Organized in April 1863. Designated as the 17th Field Artillery Battery on November 19, 1864. It was armed with three 3.40" Rifles and one 6-lb. Smoothbore in May 1865. Surrendered by General E. K. Smith, commanding Trans-Mississippi Department, on May 26, 1865.

First Commander: William Butler Krumbhaar (Captain)

Captain: W. M. Stafford

Assignments: Western Sub-district, District of Texas, New Mexico, and Arizona, Trans-Mississippi Department (April-June 1863)

Bankhead's Brigade, Bee's Division [or Western and Northern Sub-districts], District of Texas, New Mexico, and Arizona, Trans-Mississippi Department (June 1863)

Northern Sub-district, District of Texas, New Mexico, and Arizona, Trans-Mississippi Department (June-July 1863)

Bankhead's Brigade, District of the Indian Territory, Trans-Mississippi Department (November 1863)

District of the Indian Territory, Trans-Mississippi Department (November 1863-April 1864)

Gano's Brigade, Maxey's-Steele's Cavalry Division, District of Arkansas,
   Trans-Mississippi Department (April-July 1864)
7th (Krumbhaar's) Mounted Artillery Battalion, Cooper's (Indian) Cavalry
   Division, Trans-Mississippi Department (September-November 1864)
6th (Krumbhaar's) Field Artillery Battalion, 2nd (Maxey's) Texas Cavalry
   Division, 1st Corps, Trans-Mississippi Department (November 1864-May
   1865)
Battles: Camden Expedition (March-May 1864)
Poison Spring (April 18, 1864)

45.   TEXAS ABAT'S ARTILLERY BATTERY
See: TEXAS 14TH FIELD ARTILLERY BATTERY

46.   TEXAS ALAMO CITY GUARDS ARTILLERY BATTERY
See: TEXAS 1ST FIELD ARTILLERY BATTERY

47.   TEXAS AUSTIN GRAYS ARTILLERY BATTERY
Also Known As: Company B, 13th Infantry Regiment
Organization: Organized on June 14, 1863. Surrendered by General E. K.
Smith, commanding Trans-Mississippi Department, on May 26, 1865. This
battery does not appear in the *Official Records* as a separate entry. SEE: Texas
13th Infantry Regiment.
First Commander: James S. Perry (Captain)

48.   TEXAS AUSTIN LIGHT ARTILLERY
See: TEXAS 6TH FIELD ARTILLERY BATTERY

49.   TEXAS CAYCE'S-ALLEN'S ARTILLERY BATTERY
Organization: Organized in May 1862. This battery does not appear in the
Official Records.
First Commander: Henry C. Cayce (Lieutenant)
Captain: W. H. Allen

50.   TEXAS CHRISTMAS' ARTILLERY BATTERY
Organization: Organization begun at San Antonio on November 25, 1863.
Apparently failed to complete its organization and merged into Jones' Artillery
Battery in May or June 1864.
First Commander: H. H. Christmas (Captain)
Assignment: Western Sub-district, District of Texas, New Mexico, and Ari-
   zona, Trans-Mississippi Department (November 1863-May 1864)

51. TEXAS CONRAD'S ARTILLERY BATTERY

Organization: Organized on July 1, 1861. This battery does not appear in the *Official Records.*
First Commander: J. M. Conrad (Captain)

52. TEXAS COOK'S ARTILLERY BATTERY

See: TEXAS 3RD HEAVY ARTILLERY BATTALION, COMPANY A

53. TEXAS CREUZBAUR'S ARTILLERY BATTERY

See: TEXAS 5TH FIELD ARTILLERY BATTERY

54. TEXAS DALLAS ARTILLERY BATTERY

Organization: Organized in Smith and Dallas counties on July 2, 1861. It was armed with six guns from October 1861 to March 19, 1862. It was armed with two 6-lb. Smoothbores and two 12-lb. Howitzers from May 19, 1863 to March 29, 1864. It was armed with four 12-lb. Howitzers on April 1, 1864. Surrendered by Lieutenant General Richard Taylor, commanding the Department of Alabama, Mississippi, and East Louisiana, at Citronelle, Alabama on May 4, 1865.
First Commander: John J. Good (Captain)
Captain: James P. Douglas
Assignments: McCulloch's Division, Department #2 (October-December 1861)
Hébert's Brigade, McCulloch's Division, Department #2 (December 1861-January 1862)
Hébert's Brigade, McCulloch's Division, Trans-Mississippi District, Department #2 (January-February 1862)
Artillery, McCulloch's Division, Trans-Mississippi District, Department #2 (February-March 1862)
Frost's Artillery Brigade, Price's Division, Trans-Mississippi District, Department #2 (March-April 1862)
Hogg's-Cabell's Brigade, McCown's Division, Army of the West, Department #2 (April-July 1862)
Ector's Brigade, McCown's Division, Department of East Tennessee (August-December 1862)
Ector's Brigade, McCown's Division, E. K. Smith's Corps, Army of Tennessee (December 1862-February 1863)
Ector's Brigade, Stewart's Division, 1st Corps, Army of Tennessee (February-June 1863)
Churchill's Brigade, Cleburne's Division, 2nd Corps, Army of Tennessee (June-August 1863)

Artillery Battalion, Cleburne's Division, 2nd Corps, Army of Tennessee (August-November 1863)

Artillery Battalion, Hindman's Division, 2nd Corps, Army of Tennessee (November 1863-February 1864)

Courtney's Battalion, Artillery, 2nd Corps, Army of Tennessee (February 1864-January 1865)

Hoxton's Artillery Battalion, Left Wing, Defenses of Mobile, Artillery Reserves, etc., District of the Gulf, Department of Alabama, Mississippi, and East Louisiana (March-April 1865)

Hoxton's Battalion, Fuller's Artillery Regiment, Department of Alabama, Mississippi, and East Louisiana (April-May 1865)

Battles: Pea Ridge (March 7-8, 1862)

Richmond (August 30, 1862)

Murfreesboro (December 31, 1862-January 3, 1863)

Tullahoma Campaign (June 1863)

Chickamauga (September 19-20, 1863)

Chattanooga Siege (September-November 1863)

Chattanooga (November 23-25, 1863)

Ringgold Gap (November 27, 1863)

Atlanta Campaign (May-September 1864)

New Hope Church (June 27, 1864)

Atlanta Siege (July-September 1864)

Nashville (December 15-16, 1864)

Mobile (March 17-April 12, 1865)

Further Reading: Fitzhugh, Lester Newton, *Cannon Smoke: The Letters of Captain John J. Good, Good-Douglas Texas Battery, CSA.*

55.   TEXAS DANIEL'S ARTILLERY BATTERY

See: TEXAS 9TH FIELD ARTILLERY BATTERY

56.   TEXAS DASHIELL'S ARTILLERY BATTERY

See: TEXAS 14TH FIELD ARTILLERY BATTERY

57.   TEXAS DAVIS' ARTILLERY BATTERY

Organization: Organized on August 22, 1861. This battery does not appear in the *Official Records.*

First Commander: James Davis (Captain)

58.   TEXAS DEGE'S ARTILLERY BATTERY

See: TEXAS 8TH FIELD ARTILLERY BATTERY

59. TEXAS DIXIE GRAYS ARTILLERY BATTERY

See: TEXAS 3RD FIELD ARTILLERY BATTERY; TEXAS 7TH ARTILLERY BATTALION, COMPANY A; TEXAS 1ST HEAVY ARTILLERY REGIMENT, 1ST COMPANY A; TEXAS 3RD HEAVY ARTILLERY BATTALION, COMPANY A

60. TEXAS DOUGLAS' ARTILLERY BATTERY

See: TEXAS DALLAS ARTILLERY BATTERY

61. TEXAS DUKE'S ARTILLERY BATTERY

See: TEXAS JEFFERSON GUARDS ARTILLERY BATTERY

62. TEXAS EDGAR'S ARTILLERY BATTERY

See: TEXAS 1ST FIELD ARTILLERY BATTERY

63. TEXAS FONTAINE'S ARTILLERY BATTERY

See: TEXAS 3RD HEAVY ARTILLERY BATTALION, COMPANY A; TEXAS 1ST HEAVY ARTILLERY REGIMENT, 1ST COMPANY A

64. TEXAS FOX'S ARTILLERY BATTERY

See: TEXAS 8TH FIELD ARTILLERY BATTERY

65. TEXAS GALVESTON ARTILLERY BATTERY

Organization: Organized on November 25, 1861. This battery does not appear in the *Official Records*.
First Commander: H. Van Buren (Lieutenant)

66. TEXAS GIBSON'S ARTILLERY BATTERY

See: TEXAS 16TH FIELD ARTILLERY BATTERY

67. TEXAS GONZALES' ARTILLERY BATTERY

See: TEXAS 13TH FIELD ARTILLERY BATTERY

68. TEXAS GOOD'S ARTILLERY BATTERY

See: TEXAS DALLAS ARTILLERY BATTERY

69. TEXAS GUARD HORSE ARTILLERY BATTERY

See: TEXAS 17TH FIELD ARTILLERY BATTERY

70. TEXAS HALDEMAN'S ARTILLERY BATTERY
See: TEXAS 4TH FIELD ARTILLERY BATTERY

71. TEXAS HILL'S PARTISANS ARTILLERY BATTERY
Organization: Apparently failed to complete its organization during the summer of 1862.

72. TEXAS HOGUE'S ARTILLERY BATTERY
Organization: Organized on July 8, 1862. This battery does not appear in the *Official Records.*
First Commander: B. J. Hogue (Captain)

73. TEXAS HOWE'S HEAVY ARTILLERY BATTERY
Organization: Organized on June 8, 1863. Served as engineers and as sappers and miners. Became Company E, 1st Confederate Engineers Battalion on April 1, 1864.
First Commander: M. G. Howe (Captain)
Assignments: Debray's Brigade, Scurry's Division [or Eastern Sub-district], District of Texas, New Mexico, and Arizona, Trans-Mississippi Department (June 1863)
Eastern Sub-district, District of Texas, New Mexico, and Arizona, Trans-Mississippi Department (June 1863-April 1864)

74. TEXAS HOWELL'S ARTILLERY BATTERY
See: TEXAS 11TH FIELD ARTILLERY BATTERY

75. TEXAS HUGHES' ARTILLERY BATTERY
See: TEXAS 13TH FIELD ARTILLERY BATTERY

76. TEXAS HYNSON'S ARTILLERY BATTERY
See: TEXAS 10TH FIELD ARTILLERY BATTERY

77. TEXAS INDIANOLA ARTILLERY GUARD, ARTILLERY BATTERY
Organization: Organized in Calhoun County in 1861. Became Company B, 4th Artillery Battalion on December 10, 1861.
First Commander: Joseph M. Reuss (Captain)
Assignment: Department of Texas (October-December 1861)

78.   TEXAS JEFFERSON GUARDS ARTILLERY BATTERY

Organization: Organized on August 1, 1861. Disbanded in June 1862. The men were assigned to the various companies of the Texas Brigade, Army of Northern Virginia.

First Commander: W. H. Duke (Captain)

Assignments: Rains' Division, Department of the Peninsula (January-April 1862)

Artillery, Magruder's Division, Army of Northern Virginia (April-June 1862)

79.   TEXAS JONES' ARTILLERY BATTERY

See: TEXAS 3RD FIELD ARTILLERY BATTERY; TEXAS 7TH ARTILLERY BATTALION, COMPANY A; TEXAS 1ST HEAVY ARTILLERY REGIMENT, 1ST COMPANY A

80.   TEXAS KIRBY'S ARTILLERY BATTERY

Organization: Organized in October 1863. This battery does not appear in the *Official Records.*

First Commander: J. L. S. Kirby (Captain)

81.   TEXAS KRUMBHAAR'S ARTILLERY BATTERY

See: TEXAS 17TH FIELD ARTILLERY BATTERY

82.   TEXAS LAMAR ARTILLERY BATTERY

See: TEXAS 9TH FIELD ARTILLERY BATTERY

83.   TEXAS LEE'S-HUMPHREYS' ARTILLERY BATTERY

Organization: Organized in early 1863. Apparently disbanded in early 1865.

First Commander: Roswell W. Lee (Captain)

Captain: John T. Humphreys

Assignments: Cooper's Brigade, Steele's Division, District of Arkansas, Trans-Mississippi Department (April-October 1863)

Cooper's Brigade, District of the Indian Territory, Trans-Mississippi Department (October 1863-June 1864)

District of the Indian Territory, Trans-Mississippi Department (June-August 1864)

6th (Krumbhaar's) Field Artillery Battalion, 2nd (Maxey's) Texas Cavalry Division, 1st Corps, Trans-Mississippi Department (December 1864-January 1865)

Battle: near Honey Springs (July 17, 1863)

84. Texas Maclin's Artillery Battery

See: TEXAS 8TH FIELD ARTILLERY BATTERY

85. Texas Maltby's Artillery Battery

See: TEXAS NEAL'S-MALTBY'S ARTILLERY BATTERY

86. Texas Marmion's Artillery Battery

Organization: Organized in Bexar County on September 10, 1861. No further record after December 1861.

First Commander: James R. Marmion (Captain)

Assignment: Department of Texas (September-December 1861)

87. Texas Mechling's Artillery Battery

See: TEXAS 4TH FIELD ARTILLERY BATTERY

88. Texas Moseley's Artillery Battery

Organization: Organized by the conversion of Company D, 13th Infantry Regiment to artillery service on October 19, 1861. Designated as Company B, 7th Artillery Battalion in June 1863.

First Commander: William G. Moseley (Captain)

Assignments: Department of Texas (October 1861-February 1862)

Eastern District, Department of Texas (February-May 1862)

Eastern District of Texas, Trans-Mississippi Department (May-August 1862)

District of Texas, Trans-Mississippi Department (August-December 1862)

District of Texas, New Mexico, and Arizona, Trans-Mississippi Department (December 1862-January 1863)

Eastern Sub-district, District of Texas, New Mexico, and Arizona, Trans-Mississippi Department (January-June 1863)

Battle: Galveston Island (January 1, 1863)

89. Texas Neal's-Maltby's Artillery Battery

Organization: Organized on October 24, 1861. Captured on Mustang Island off Corpus Christie on November 17, 1863.

First Commander: B. F. Neal (Captain)

Captain: William N. Maltby

Assignments: Department of Texas (October 1861-February 1862)

Western District, Department of Texas (February-May 1862)

Western District of Texas, Trans-Mississippi Department (May-August 1862)

District of Texas, Trans-Mississippi Department (August-December 1862)

District of Texas, New Mexico, and Arizona, Trans-Mississippi Department
(December 1862-January 1863)
Western Sub-district, District of Texas, New Mexico, and Arizona, Trans-Mississippi Department (January-November 1863)
Battles: Corpus Christie (August 16-18, 1862)
Mustang Island (November 17, 1863)

90. TEXAS NETTLES' ARTILLERY BATTERY
See: TEXAS 12TH FIELD ARTILLERY BATTERY

91. TEXAS NICHOLS' ARTILLERY BATTERY
See: TEXAS 15TH FIELD ARTILLERY BATTERY; TEXAS 1ST HEAVY ARTILLERY REGIMENT, COMPANY D

92. TEXAS PRATT'S ARTILLERY BATTERY
See: TEXAS 10TH FIELD ARTILLERY BATTERY

93. TEXAS RANSOM'S ARTILLERY BATTERY
See: TEXAS 1ST FIELD ARTILLERY BATTERY

94. TEXAS REILY'S HOWITZER ARTILLERY BATTERY
Organization: Organized by details from the 4th Cavalry Regiment and attached to that regiment on December 17, 1861. Disbanded in early 1862.
First Commander: John Reily (Lieutenant)
Assignments: Sibley's Brigade (December 1861)
Army of New Mexico (December 1861-April 1862)
Battle: Valverde (February 21, 1862)
Further Reading: Hall, Martin Hardwick, *Sibley's New Mexico Campaign.*

95. TEXAS ROCKET ARTILLERY BATTERY
Organization: Organized in late 1863. Reorganized as a rocket battery in March 1864. Disbanded in the spring of 1864.
First Commander: John S. Greer (Captain)
Assignments: Western Sub-district, District of Texas, New Mexico, and Arizona, Trans-Mississippi Department (December 1863-January 1864)
Eastern Sub-district, District of Texas, New Mexico, and Arizona, Trans-Mississippi Department (January-February 1864)
Duff's Brigade, Bee's Division [or Western and Northern Sub-districts], District of Texas, New Mexico, and Arizona, Trans-Mississippi Department (February-March 1864)

Western Sub-district, District of Texas, New Mexico, and Arizona, Trans-Mississippi Department (April 1864)

96.   TEXAS SAYERS' ARTILLERY BATTERY
See: TEXAS 12TH FIELD ARTILLERY BATTERY

97.   TEXAS SHEA'S ARTILLERY BATTALION,
See: TEXAS 4TH ARTILLERY BATTALION

98.   TEXAS SHEA'S ARTILLERY BATTERY
Organization: Organized on July 19, 1861. Became Company A, 4th Artillery Battalion on December 10, 1861.
First Commander: Daniel D. Shea (Captain)
Assignment: Department of Texas (July-December 1861)

99.   TEXAS STAFFORD'S ARTILLERY BATTERY
See: TEXAS 17TH FIELD ARTILLERY BATTERY

100.   TEXAS TEEL'S-BENNETT'S ARTILLERY BATTERY
Also Known As: Company B, 1st Heavy Artillery Regiment
Organization: Organized on May 1, 1861. Apparently disbanded in the spring of 1862.
First Commander: Trevanion T. Teel (Captain)
Captain: Jordan W. Bennett
Assignments: Sibley's Brigade (September-December 1861)
Army of New Mexico (December 1861-December 1862)
Battles: San Lucas Springs (May 9, 1861)
New Mexico Campaign (January-April 1862)
Valverde (February 21, 1862)

101.   TEXAS GUARDS ARTILLERY BATTERY
See: TEXAS 17TH FIELD ARTILLERY BATTERY

102.   TEXAS VALVERDE ARTILLERY BATTERY
See: TEXAS 12TH FIELD ARTILLERY BATTERY

103.   TEXAS VAN DORN LIGHT ARTILLERY BATTERY
See: TEXAS 4TH FIELD ARTILLERY BATTERY

104. TEXAS WAUL'S LEGION ARTILLERY BATTERY
See: TEXAS 1ST FIELD ARTILLERY BATTERY

105. TEXAS WILLKE'S ARTILLERY BATTALION
First Commander: H. Willke (Major)

106. TEXAS WILLKE'S ARTILLERY BATTALION, COMPANY A
See: TEXAS 5TH FIELD ARTILLERY BATTERY

107. TEXAS WILLKE'S ARTILLERY BATTALION, COMPANY C
Organization: Organized in 1863.
Assignment: Western Sub-district, District of Texas, New Mexico, and Arizona, Trans-Mississippi Department (September-October 1863)

108. TEXAS WILLKE'S ARTILLERY BATTALION, COMPANY D
Organization: Organized in 1863.
Assignment: Western Sub-district, District of Texas, New Mexico, and Arizona, Trans-Mississippi Department (September-October 1863)

109. TEXAS WILSON'S-GONZALES'-HUGHES' ARTILLERY BATTERY
See: TEXAS 13TH FIELD ARTILLERY BATTERY

110. TEXAS WOOD'S HOWITZER ARTILLERY BATTERY
Organization: Organized by details from the 5th Cavalry Regiment and attached to that regiment in September 1861. Disbanded in July 1862.
First Commander: William S. Wood (Lieutenant)
Assignments: Sibley's Brigade (September-December 1861)
Army of New Mexico (December 1861-July 1862)
Battles: New Mexico Campaign (January-April 1862)
Valverde (February 21, 1862)
Further Reading: Hall, Martin Hardwick, *Sibley's New Mexico Campaign.*

CAVALRY

111. TEXAS 1ST CAVALRY BATTALION

Organization: Organized in 1861. Mustered into Confederate service at Jefferson, Marion County in mid-November 1861. Dismounted in April 1862. Increased to a regiment and designated as the 32nd Cavalry Regiment in May 1862.

First Commander: R. P. Crump (Major, Lieutenant Colonel)

Assignments: Department of Texas (November 1861)

Unattached, Trans-Mississippi District, Department #2 (March 1862)

Greer's Cavalry Brigade, Price's Division, Trans-Mississippi District, Department #2 (March-April 1862)

Hogg's Brigade, McCown's Division, Army of the West, Department #2 (April-May 1862)

Battles: Pea Ridge (March 7-8, 1862)

Corinth Campaign (April-June 1862)

112. TEXAS 1ST CAVALRY BATTALION, ARIZONA BRIGADE

Also Known As: 4th Cavalry Battalion, Arizona Brigade

Organization: Organized with four companies in early 1863. Apparently merged into the 1st Cavalry Regiment, Arizona Brigade in January 1865.

First Commander: A. H. Davidson (Major, Lieutenant Colonel)

Field Officer: Michael Looscan (Major)

Assignments: Eastern Sub-district, District of Texas, New Mexico, and Arizona, Trans-Mississippi Department (February-June 1863)

Northern Sub-district, District of Texas, New Mexico, and Arizona, Trans-Mississippi Department (July 1863)

Eastern Sub-district, District of Texas, New Mexico, and Arizona, Trans-Mississippi Department (August-November 1863)

Buckel's Brigade, District of Texas, Eastern Sub-district, New Mexico, and Arizona, Trans-Mississippi Department (November-December 1863)

Buchel's Cavalry Brigade, Slaughter's Division [or Eastern Sub-district], District of Texas, New Mexico, and Arizona, Trans-Mississippi Department (December 1863-January 1864)

113. TEXAS 1ST CAVALRY BATTALION, STATE TROOPS

Organization: Organized for six months in late 1863. Mustered out in early 1864.
First Commander: D. D. Holland (Lieutenant Colonel)
Field Officer: Joseph Taylor (Major)
Assignments: Gillespie's Cavalry Brigade, Slaughter's Division [or Eastern Sub-district], District of Texas, New Mexico, and Arizona, Trans-Mississippi Department (December 1863-January 1864)
Eastern Sub-district, District of Texas, New Mexico, and Arizona, Trans-Mississippi Department (January 1864)

114. TEXAS 1ST CAVALRY REGIMENT

Organization: Organized by the consolidation of the 3rd and 8th Cavalry Battalions ca. May 1863. Dismounted in late 1863. Subsequently remounted. Surrendered by General E. K. Smith, commanding Trans-Mississippi Department, on May 26, 1865. Disbanded at Wild Cat Bluff ca. May 27, 1865.
First Commander: Augustus Buchel (Colonel)
Field Officers: Robert A. Myers (Major)
William O. Yager (Lieutenant Colonel)
Assignments: Western Sub-district, District of Texas, New Mexico, and Arizona, Trans-Mississippi Department (February-June 1863)
1st Brigade, Bee's Division [or Western Sub-district], District of Texas, New Mexico, and Arizona, Trans-Mississippi Department (June-August 1863)
Eastern Sub-district, District of Texas, New Mexico, and Arizona, Trans-Mississippi Department (August-September 1863)
Buchel's Brigade, Slaughter's Division [or Eastern Sub-district], District of Texas, New Mexico, and Arizona, Trans-Mississippi Department (September 1863-January 1864)
Eastern Sub-district, District of Texas, New Mexico, and Arizona, Trans-Mississippi Department (January-March 1864)
Hawes'-Bagby's Brigade, Green's Cavalry Division, District of West Louisiana, Trans-Mississippi Department (March-September 1864)
4th (Bagby's) Texas Cavalry Brigade, 2nd (Maxey's) Texas Cavalry Division, 1st Corps, Trans-Mississippi Department (September 1864-May 1865)
Battles: Matagorda Peninsula [skirmish] (December 29, 1863)
Caney Bayou, Texas Bombardment (January 8-9, 1864)
Los Patricios [one company] (March 13, 1864)

Corpus Christie [one company] (March 17, 1864)
Red River Campaign (March-May 1864)
Mansfield (April 8, 1864)
Pleasant Hill (April 9, 1864)
near Moreauville (May 17, 1864)
Eagle Pass [one company] (June 19, 1864)
Atchafalaya River (September 17, 1864)
Bayou Ala and Morgan's Ferry (September 20, 1864)
Further Reading: Spencer, John W., *Terrell's Texas Cavalry.* Gautier, George R., *Harder Than Death, The Life of George R. Gautier, an Old Texan, Living at the Confederate Home, Austin, Texas.*

115.   TEXAS 1ST CAVALRY REGIMENT, ARIZONA BRIGADE

Also Known As: 31st Cavalry Regiment
Organization: Organized by the increase of Hardeman's Cavalry Battalion, Arizona Brigade to a regiment on February 21, 1863, per S.O. #81, District of Texas, New Mexico, and Arizona, Trans-Mississippi Department. Dismounted in March 1865. Surrendered by General E. K. Smith, commanding Trans-Mississippi Department, on May 26, 1865.
First Commander: William P. Hardeman (Colonel)
Field Officers: Peter Hardeman (Lieutenant Colonel, Colonel)
Michael Looscan (Major)
Edward Riordan (Lieutenant Colonel)
Alexander W. Terrell (Major)
Assignments: Western Sub-district, District of Texas, New Mexico, and Arizona, Trans-Mississippi Department (February-May 1863)
Bankhead's Brigade, Bee's Division [or Western Sub-district], District of Texas, New Mexico, and Arizona, Trans-Mississippi Department (May-June 1863)
Northern Sub-district, District of Texas, New Mexico, and Arizona, Trans-Mississippi Department (June-July 1863)
Indian Territory, District of Arkansas, Trans-Mississippi Department (July-August 1863)
Northern Sub-district, District of Texas, New Mexico, and Arizona, Trans-Mississippi Department (October 1863-January 1864)
Gano's Brigade, Maxey's Cavalry Division, District of Arkansas, Trans-Mississippi Department (April-July 1864)
Gano's Brigade, District of the Indian Territory, Trans-Mississippi Department (July-August 1864)
Gano's Brigade, Cooper's (Indian) Division, District of the Indian Territory, Trans-Mississippi Department (September 1864)

5th (Gano's) Texas Cavalry Brigade, 2nd (Maxey's) Texas Cavalry Division, 1st Corps, Trans-Mississippi Department (September 1864-January 1865)

Harrison's Brigade, Maxey's Division, District of Texas, New Mexico, and Arizona, Trans-Mississippi Department (April-May 1865)

Battles: Camden Expedition (March-May 1864)

Poison Spring (April 18, 1864)

Massard's Prairie, near Fort Smith [detachment] (July 27, 1864)

Cabin Creek (September 19, 1864)

116.   TEXAS 1ST CAVALRY REGIMENT, LANCERS

See: TEXAS 21ST CAVALRY REGIMENT

117.   TEXAS 1ST CAVALRY REGIMENT, MOUNTED RIFLES

Organization: Organized for 12 months on April 15, 1861. Mustered into state service ca. April 1861. Reduced to a battalion of five companies and designated as the 8th Cavalry Battalion ca. April 1862.

First Commander: Henry E. McCulloch (Colonel)

Field Officers: John B. Barry (Major)

Edward Burleson, Jr. (Major)

Thomas C. Frost (Lieutenant Colonel)

Assignments: Department of Texas (April 1861-February 1862)

Western Sub-district, Department of Texas (February-April 1862)

Battles: San Lucas Springs [six companies] (May 9, 1861)

Peosi River *vs.* Indians [one company] (November 1, 1861)

118.   TEXAS 1ST CAVALRY REGIMENT, PARTISAN RANGERS

Organization: Organized in the fall of 1862. Surrendered by General E. K. Smith, commanding Trans-Mississippi Department, on May 26, 1865.

First Commander: Walter P. Lane (Colonel)

Field Officers: A. D. Burns (Major)

R. P. Crump (Lieutenant Colonel)

William P. Saufley (Major)

Assignments: Department of the Indian Territory (October 1862)

MacDonald's Brigade, Marmaduke's Cavalry Division, 1st Corps, Trans-Mississippi Department (November-December 1862)

Cooper's Brigade, Roane's Division, 1st Corps, Trans-Mississippi Department (December 1862-January 1863)

Department of the Indian Territory (January 1863)

Major's Brigade, Green's Cavalry Division, Sub-district of Southwestern Louisiana, District of West Louisiana, Trans-Mississippi Department (May-December 1863)

Major's Brigade, Green's Cavalry Division, Eastern Sub-district, District of Texas, New Mexico, and Arizona, Trans-Mississippi Department (December 1863-February 1864)

Major's Brigade, Green's Cavalry Division, District of West Louisiana, Trans-Mississippi Department (March-September 1864)

2nd (Major's) Texas Cavalry Brigade, 1st (Wharton's) Texas Cavalry Division, 2nd Corps, Trans-Mississippi Department (September 1864-March 1865)

Hardeman's Brigade, Bee's Division, Wharton's Cavalry Corps, Trans-Mississippi Department (March-May 1865)

Battles: Prairie Grove (December 7, 1862)

Donaldsonville (June 28, 1863)

Cox's Plantation (July 12-13, 1863)

Stirling's Plantation [in reserve] (September 29, 1863)

Bayou Bourbeau (November 3, 1863)

Red River Campaign (March-May 1864)

Mansfield (April 8, 1864)

Pleasant Hill (April 9, 1864)

Monticello (September 10, 1864)

119. TEXAS 1ST CAVALRY REGIMENT, STATE TROOPS

Organization: Organized for six months in late 1863. Mustered out in early 1864.

First Commander: Tignal W. Jones (Colonel)

Field Officers: J. G. Coleman (Major)

G. W. Stidham (Lieutenant Colonel)

Assignments: Eastern Sub-district, District of Texas, New Mexico, and Arizona, Trans-Mississippi Department (December 1863)

Gillespie's Cavalry Brigade, Slaughter's Division [or Eastern Sub-district], District of Texas, New Mexico, and Arizona, Trans-Mississippi Department (December 1863-January 1864)

120. TEXAS 1ST TEXAS LEGION CAVALRY REGIMENT

See: TEXAS 27TH CAVALRY REGIMENT

121. TEXAS 1ST TEXAS RANGERS CAVALRY REGIMENT

See: TEXAS 8TH CAVALRY REGIMENT

122. TEXAS 1ST (GURLEY'S) CAVALRY REGIMENT, PARTISAN RANGERS

See: TEXAS 30TH CAVALRY REGIMENT

123. TEXAS 1ST "INDIAN-TEXAS" CAVALRY REGIMENT
See: TEXAS 22ND CAVALRY REGIMENT

124. TEXAS 2ND CAVALRY BATTALION, ARIZONA BRIGADE
Organization: Organized with six companies in early 1863. Consolidated with two companies of Mullen's Cavalry Battalion, Arizona Brigade, and two independent companies and designated as the 2nd Cavalry Regiment, Arizona Brigade on February 21, 1863, per S.O. #81, District of Texas, New Mexico, and Arizona, Trans-Mississippi Department.
First Commander: George W. Baylor (Lieutenant Colonel)
Assignment: Eastern Sub-district, District of Texas, New Mexico, and Arizona, Trans-Mississippi Department (February 1863)

125. TEXAS 2ND CAVALRY BATTALION, STATE TROOPS
Organization: Organized with three companies for six months in late 1863. Increased to a regiment and designated as the 2nd Cavalry Regiment, State Troops in late 1863.
First Commander: J. C. Carter (Major)
Assignments: Northern Sub-district, District of Texas, New Mexico, and Arizona, Trans-Mississippi Department (November 1863)
Townes' Cavalry Brigade, Slaughter's Division [or Eastern Sub-district], District of Texas, New Mexico, and Arizona, Trans-Mississippi Department (December 1863-January 1864)

126. TEXAS 2ND CAVALRY REGIMENT
Also Known As: 2nd Mounted Rifles
Organization: Organized as the 2nd Mounted Rifles in the spring of 1861. Reorganized as the 2nd Cavalry Regiment in the spring of 1862. Dismounted in early 1863, having apparently mutinied in mid-1862. Punishment revoked and the regiment was reorganized at Austin in September 1863. Dismounted in March 1865. Surrendered by General E. K. Smith, commanding Trans-Mississippi Department, on May 26, 1865.
First Commander: John S. "Rip" Ford (Colonel)
Field Officers: John R. Baylor (Lieutenant Colonel)
John Donelson (Major)
Matthew Nolan (Major)
Charles L. Pyron (Major, Lieutenant Colonel, Colonel)
William A. Spencer (Major, Lieutenant Colonel)
James Walker (Lieutenant Colonel)
Edward Waller, Jr. (Major)
Assignments: Department of Texas (April-September 1861)

Sibley's Brigade (September-December 1861)

Army of New Mexico (December 1861-April 1862)

Western District of Texas, Department of Texas (May 1862)

Western District of Texas, Trans-Mississippi Department (May-August 1862)

District of Texas, Trans-Mississippi Department (August-October 1862)

Sub-district of the Rio Grande, District of Texas, Trans-Mississippi Department (October-November 1862)

Sub-district of Houston, District of Texas, Trans-Mississippi Department (November 1862)

District of Texas, New Mexico, and Arizona, Trans-Mississippi Department (December 1862-January 1863)

Eastern Sub-district, District of Texas, New Mexico, and Arizona, Trans-Mississippi Department (January-May 1863)

Major's Cavalry Brigade, District of West Louisiana, Trans-Mississippi Department (June-July 1863)

Eastern Sub-district, District of Texas, New Mexico, and Arizona, Trans-Mississippi Department (August-November 1863)

Debray's Command, Eastern Sub-district, District of Texas, New Mexico, and Arizona, Trans-Mississippi Department (November-December 1863)

Duff's Brigade, Bee's Division [or Western Sub-district], District of Texas, New Mexico, and Arizona, Trans-Mississippi Department (December 1863-January 1864)

Western Sub-district, District of Texas, New Mexico, and Arizona, Trans-Mississippi Department (January-June 1864)

1st [or Eastern] Sub-district, District of Texas, New Mexico, and Arizona, Trans-Mississippi Department (July-September 1864)

7th (Slaughter's) Texas Cavalry Brigade, 3rd (Drayton's) Texas Cavalry Division, 3rd Corps, Trans-Mississippi Department (September 1864-May 1865)

Battles: San Lucas Springs [squadron] (May 9, 1861)

Mesilla (July 25, 1861)

San Augustine Springs (July 27, 1861)

Fort Stanton (August 2, 1861)

Fort Craig (August 25, 1861)

Operations about Fort Stanton *vs.* Indians [Company D] (August 25-September 8, 1861)

near Fort Bliss *vs.* Indians [skirmish] [detachment] (August 1861)

Fort Thorn [detachments of Companies A, B, & E] (August 26, 1861)

Cañada Alamosa [detachments of Companies A, B, & E] (September 25, 1861)

Operations from Camp Robledo *vs.* Indians [detachment Company A] (September 30-October 7, 1861)

Operations from Fort Inge *vs*. Indians [detachment Company A] (October 11-16, 1861)
New Mexico Campaign (January-April 1862)
Valverde (February 21, 1862)
Nueces River, near Fort Clark (August 10, 1862)
Galveston Island (January 1, 1863)
Attack on Blockading Squadron at Sabine Pass (January 21, 1863)

127. TEXAS 2ND CAVALRY REGIMENT, ARIZONA BRIGADE

Organization: Organized by the consolidation of the 2nd Cavalry Battalion, Arizona Brigade, two companies of Mullen's Cavalry Battalion, Arizona Brigade, and two independent companies on February 21, 1863, per S.O. #81, District of Texas, New Mexico, and Arizona, Trans-Mississippi Department. Dismounted in March 1865. Surrendered by General E. K. Smith, commanding Trans-Mississippi Department, on May 26, 1865.
First Commander: George W. Baylor (Colonel)
Field Officers: Sherod Hunter (Major)
John W. Mullen (Lieutenant Colonel)
Assignments: Eastern Sub-district, District of Texas, New Mexico, and Arizona, Trans-Mississippi Department (February-April 1863)
Green's Cavalry Brigade, Mouton's Command, District of West Louisiana, Trans-Mississippi Department (May-December 1863)
Major's Brigade, Green's Cavalry Division, District of West Louisiana, Trans-Mississippi Department (December 1863)
Major's Brigade, Green's Cavalry Division, Eastern Sub-district, District of Texas, New Mexico, and Arizona, Trans-Mississippi Department (December 1863-February 1864)
Major's Brigade, Green's Cavalry Division, District of West Louisiana, Trans-Mississippi Department (March-September 1864)
2nd (Major's) Texas Cavalry Brigade, 1st (Wharton's) Texas Cavalry Division, 2nd Corps, Trans-Mississippi Department (September 1864-March 1865)
Robertson's Brigade, Maxey's Division, District of Texas, New Mexico, and Arizona, Trans-Mississippi Department (April-May 1865)
Battles: Brashear City (June 23, 1863)
Cox's Plantation (July 12-13, 1863)
Red River Campaign (March-May 1864)
Mansfield (April 8, 1864)
Pleasant Hill (April 9, 1864)

128. TEXAS 2ND CAVALRY REGIMENT, LANCERS

See: TEXAS 24TH CAVALRY REGIMENT

129. TEXAS 2ND CAVALRY REGIMENT, MOUNTED RIFLES
See: TEXAS 2ND CAVALRY REGIMENT

130. TEXAS 2ND CAVALRY REGIMENT, PARTISAN RANGERS
Organization: Organized in early 1863. Dismounted in February 1865. Surrendered by General E. K. Smith, commanding Trans-Mississippi Department, on May 26, 1865.
First Commander: B. Warren Stone (Colonel)
Field Officers: Isham Chisum (Lieutenant Colonel, Colonel)
Crill Miller (Lieutenant Colonel)
James W. Throckmorton (Major)
James G. Vance (Major)
Assignments: Major's Brigade, Green's Cavalry Division, Sub-district of Southwestern Louisiana, District of West Louisiana, Trans-Mississippi Department (May-December 1863)
Major's Brigade, Green's Cavalry Division, Eastern Sub-district, District of Texas, New Mexico, and Arizona, Trans-Mississippi Department (December 1863-February 1864)
Major's Brigade, Green's Cavalry Division, District of West Louisiana, Trans-Mississippi Department (March-September 1864)
2nd (Major's) Texas Cavalry Brigade, 1st (Wharton's) Texas Cavalry Division, 2nd Corps, Trans-Mississippi Department (September 1864-February 1865)
2nd (Waterhouse's) Texas Infantry Brigade, 1st (Forney's) Texas Infantry Division, 1st Corps, Trans-Mississippi Department (February-May 1865)
Battles: Donaldsonville (June 28, 1863)
Stirling's Plantation [in reserve] (September 29, 1863)
Bayou Bourbeau (November 3, 1863)
Red River Campaign (March-May 1864)
Mansfield (April 8, 1864)
Pleasant Hill (April 9, 1864)

131. TEXAS 2ND CAVALRY REGIMENT, STATE TROOPS
Organization: Organized by the increase of the 2nd Cavalry Battalion, State Troops to a regiment in late 1863. Mustered out in early 1864.
First Commander: Gideon Smith (Colonel)
Field Officers: J. C. Carter (Lieutenant Colonel)
James B. McLean (Major)
Assignment: Townes' Cavalry Brigade, Slaughter's Division [or Eastern Sub-district], District of Texas, New Mexico, and Arizona, Trans-Mississippi Department (December 1863-January 1864)

132. TEXAS 2ND (ALEXANDER'S) CAVALRY REGIMENT, PARTISAN RANGERS

See: TEXAS 34TH (ALEXANDER'S) CAVALRY REGIMENT

133. TEXAS 2ND (STONE'S) CAVALRY REGIMENT

See: TEXAS 6TH CAVALRY REGIMENT

134. TEXAS 3RD CAVALRY BATTALION

Organization: Organized with five companies in late 1861. Consolidated with the 8th Cavalry Battalion and designated as the 1st Cavalry Regiment ca. May 1863.

First Commander: William O. Yager (Major)

Assignments: Western District of Texas, Department of Texas (February-May 1862)

Western District of Texas, Trans-Mississippi Department (May-August 1862)

District of Texas, Trans-Mississippi Department (August-October 1862)

Sub-district of the Rio Grande, District of Texas, Trans-Mississippi Department (October-December 1862)

Sub-district of the Rio Grande, District of Texas, New Mexico, and Arizona, Trans-Mississippi Department (December 1862-January 1863)

Western Sub-district, District of Texas, New Mexico, and Arizona, Trans-Mississippi Department (January-February 1863)

Battle: Aransas Bay (April 22, 1862)

Further Reading: Spencer, John W., *Terrell's Texas Cavalry.*

135. TEXAS 3RD CAVALRY BATTALION, ARIZONA BRIGADE

Organization: Organized in early 1863. Increased to a regiment and designated as the 3rd Cavalry Regiment, Arizona Brigade on February 21, 1863, per S.O. #81, District of Texas, New Mexico, and Arizona, Trans-Mississippi Department.

First Commander: George T. Madison (Lieutenant Colonel)

Assignments: District of Texas, New Mexico, and Arizona, Trans-Mississippi Department (February 1863)

Western Sub-district, District of Texas, New Mexico, and Arizona, Trans-Mississippi Department (February 1863)

136. TEXAS 3RD CAVALRY BATTALION, STATE TROOPS

Organization: Organized in late 1863. Mustered out in early 1864.

First Commander: John M. Morin (Lieutenant Colonel)

Field Officer: L. G. Scoggins (Major)

Assignment: Anderson's Brigade, Slaughter's Division [or Eastern Sub-district], District of Texas, New Mexico, and Arizona, Trans-Mississippi Department (December 1863-January 1864)

137. TEXAS 3RD CAVALRY REGIMENT

Nickname: South Kansas-Texas Regiment

Organization: Organized at Dallas on June 13, 1861. Mustered into Confederate service at Dallas on June 13, 1861. Dismounted in April 1862. Remounted in late October 1862. Surrendered by Lieutenant General Richard Taylor, commanding the Department of Alabama, Mississippi, and East Louisiana, at Citronelle, Alabama on May 4, 1865.

First Commander: Elkanah Greer (Colonel)

Field Officers: J. J. A. Barker (Major)

Giles S. Boggess (Major, Lieutenant Colonel)

George W. Chilton (Major)

Robert H. Cumby (Lieutenant Colonel, Colonel)

J. A. Harris (Major)

Walter P. Lane (Lieutenant Colonel)

Hinchie P. Mabry (Lieutenant Colonel, Colonel)

Absalom B. Stone (Major)

Assignments: Department of Texas (June 1861)

Indian Territory (July 1861)

McCulloch's Brigade (July-August 1861)

Indian Territory (August-September 1861)

McCulloch's Division, Department #2 (September 1861-January 1862)

McIntosh's Brigade, McCulloch's Division, Department #2 (January 1862)

McIntosh's Brigade, McCulloch's Division, Trans-Mississippi District, Department #2 (January-March 1862)

Greer's Cavalry Brigade, Price's Division, Trans-Mississippi District, Department #2 (March-April 1862)

Greer's Cavalry Brigade, Army of the West, Department #2 (April 1862)

Hébert's Brigade, Price's-Little's Division, Army of the West, Department #2 (April-July 1862)

Hébert's Brigade, Little's-Hébert's-Green's Division, Price's Corps, Army of West Tennessee, Department #2 (September-October 1862)

Griffith's-Whitfield's Cavalry Brigade, Maury's Division, Price's Corps, Army of West Tennessee, Department of Mississippi and East Louisiana (October-December 1862)

Whitfield's Brigade, 2nd Division, Van Dorn's Cavalry Corps, Department of Mississippi and East Louisiana (January-February 1863)

Whitfield's Brigade, Jackson's Division, Van Dorn's Cavalry Corps, Department of Mississippi and East Louisiana (February 1863)

Whitfield's Brigade, Jackson's Division, Van Dorn's Cavalry Corps, Army of Tennessee (February-May 1863)

Whitfield's Brigade, Jackson's Cavalry Division, Department of the West (June-July 1863)

Whitfield's Brigade, Jackson's Cavalry Division, Department of Mississippi and East Louisiana (July-August 1863)

Whitfield's-Ross' Brigade, Jackson's Division, Lee's Cavalry Corps, Department of Mississippi and East Louisiana (August 1863-January 1864)

Ross' Brigade, Jackson's Division, Lee's Cavalry Corps, Department of Alabama, Mississippi, and East Louisiana (January-May 1864)

Ross' Brigade, Jackson's Cavalry Division, Army of Mississippi (May-July 1864)

Ross' Brigade, Jackson's Cavalry Division, Army of Tennessee (July 1864-February 1865)

Ross' Brigade, Jackson's Division, Forrest's Cavalry Corps, Department of Alabama, Mississippi, and East Louisiana (February-May 1865)

Battles: Wilson's Creek (August 10, 1861)

Chustenahlah, Indian Territory [five companies] (December 26, 1861)

Pea Ridge (March 7-8, 1862)

Corinth Campaign (April-June 1862)

Iuka (September 19, 1862)

Corinth (October 3-4, 1862)

Oakland [skirmish] (December 3, 1862)

Holly Springs (December 20, 1862)

Davis' Mills (December 21, 1862)

Thompson's Station (March 5, 1863)

Vicksburg Campaign (May-July 1863)

Jackson Siege (July 1863)

Middleburg (December 24, 1862)

Meridian Campaign (February-March 1864)

Snyder's Bluff (March 30, 1864)

Marion County (April 19, 1864)

Atlanta Campaign (May-September 1864)

Atlanta Siege (July-September 1864)

Flat Shoals (July 28, 1864)

Brown's Mill (July 30, 1864)

Newnan (July 30, 1864)

Franklin-Nashville Campaign (October 1864-January 1865)

Further Reading: Barron, Samuel Benton, *The Lone Star Defenders, A Chronicle of the Third Texas Cavalry, Ross' Brigade.*

138. TEXAS 3RD CAVALRY REGIMENT, ARIZONA BRIGADE

Organization: Organized by the increase of the 3rd Cavalry Battalion, Arizona Brigade to a regiment on February 21, 1863, per S.O. #81, District of Texas, New Mexico, and Arizona, Trans-Mississippi Department. Surrendered by General E. K. Smith, commanding Trans-Mississippi Department, on May 26, 1865.

First Commander: Joseph Phillips (Colonel)

Field Officers: George T. Madison (Lieutenant Colonel)

Alonzo Ridley (Major)

Assignments: Eastern Sub-district, District of Texas, New Mexico, and Arizona, Trans-Mississippi Department (February-April 1863)

Green's Brigade, Green's Cavalry Division, Sub-district of Southwestern Louisiana, District of West Louisiana, Trans-Mississippi Department (May-December 1863)

Major's Brigade, Green's Cavalry Division, District of West Louisiana, Trans-Mississippi Department (December 1863)

Major's Brigade, Green's Cavalry Division, Eastern Sub-district, District of Texas, New Mexico, and Arizona, Trans-Mississippi Department (December 1863-February 1864)

Major's Brigade, Green's Cavalry Division, District of West Louisiana, Trans-Mississippi Department (March-September 1864)

2nd (Major's) Texas Cavalry Brigade, 1st (Wharton's) Texas Cavalry Division, 2nd Corps, Trans-Mississippi Department (September 1864-February 1865)

Lane's Brigade, Bee's Division, Wharton's Cavalry Corps, Trans-Mississippi Department (February-May 1865)

Battles: Donaldsonville (June 28, 1863)

Cox's Plantation (July 12-13, 1863)

Stirling's Plantation (September 29, 1863)

Bayou Bourbeau (November 3, 1863)

Red River Campaign (March-May 1864)

Mansfield (April 8, 1864)

Pleasant Hill (April 9, 1864)

139. TEXAS 3RD CAVALRY REGIMENT, LANCERS

See: TEXAS 25TH CAVALRY REGIMENT

140. TEXAS 3RD CAVALRY REGIMENT, STATE TROOPS

Organization: Organized for six months in late 1863. Mustered out in early 1864.

First Commander: T. J. M. Richardson (Colonel)

Field Officers: George O. Dunaway (Lieutenant Colonel)

L. M. Rogers (Major)

Assignments: Western Sub-district, District of Texas, New Mexico, and Arizona, Trans-Mississippi Department (November-December 1863)

Duff's Cavalry Brigade, Bee's Division [or Western Sub-district], District of Texas, New Mexico, and Arizona, Trans-Mississippi Department (December 1863-January 1864)

141. TEXAS 4TH CAVALRY BATTALION

Organization: Organized with five companies in the fall of 1861. Increased to a regiment of 12 companies and designated as the 27th Cavalry Regiment in early 1862.

First Commander: John W. Whitfield (Major)

Assignments: McCulloch's Division, Department #2 (October-December 1861)

Hébert's Brigade, McCulloch's Division, Department #2 (December 1861-January 1862)

Hébert's Brigade, McCulloch's Division, Trans-Mississippi District, Department #2 (January-February 1862)

Unattached, Trans-Mississippi District, Department #2 (March 1862)

Hébert's Brigade, Price's Division, Trans-Mississippi District, Department #2 (March 1862)

Battle: Pea Ridge (March 7-8, 1862)

142. TEXAS 4TH CAVALRY BATTALION, ARIZONA BRIGADE

See: TEXAS 1ST CAVALRY BATTALION, ARIZONA BRIGADE

143. TEXAS 4TH CAVALRY BATTALION, STATE TROOPS

Organization: Organized for six months in late 1863. Mustered out in early 1864.

First Commander: Charles W. Tait (Major, Lieutenant Colonel)

Field Officer: Eggleston D. Townes (Major)

Assignments: Eastern Sub-district, District of Texas, New Mexico, and Arizona, Trans-Mississippi Department (October-December 1863)

Anderson's Brigade, Slaughter's Division [or Eastern Sub-district], District of Texas, New Mexico, and Arizona, Trans-Mississippi Department (December 1863-January 1864)

144. TEXAS 4TH CAVALRY REGIMENT

Also Known As: Reily's Cavalry Regiment

Organization: Organized in September 1861. Surrendered by General E. K. Smith, commanding Trans-Mississippi Department, on May 26, 1865.

First Commander: James Reily (Colonel)

Field Officers: George J. Hampton (Major, Lieutenant Colonel)
William P. Hardeman (Lieutenant Colonel, Colonel)
Charles M. Lesueur (Major)
Henry W. Raguet (Major)
William R. Scurry (Lieutenant Colonel)
Assignments: Sibley's Brigade (September-December 1861)
Army of New Mexico (December 1861-December 1862)
Sibley's-Green's Cavalry Brigade, District of Texas, New Mexico, and Arizona,
    Trans-Mississippi Department (December 1862-January 1863)
Green's Cavalry Brigade, Eastern Sub-district, District of Texas, New Mexico,
    and Arizona, Trans-Mississippi Department (January 1863)
Green's Cavalry Brigade, District of West Louisiana, Trans-Mississippi Depart-
    ment (March-May 1863)
Green's-Bagby's Brigade, Green's Cavalry Division, Sub-district of Southwest-
    ern Louisiana, District of West Louisiana, Trans-Mississippi Department
    (May-December 1863)
Green's-Bagby's Brigade, Green's Cavalry Division, Eastern Sub-district, Dis-
    trict of Texas, New Mexico, and Arizona, Trans-Mississippi Department
    (December 1863-March 1864)
Green's-Bagby's Brigade, Green's-Wharton's Cavalry Division, District of West
    Louisiana, Trans-Mississippi Department (March-September 1864)
3rd (Hardeman's) Texas Cavalry Brigade, 1st (Wharton's) Texas Cavalry
    Division, 2nd Corps, Trans-Mississippi Department (September 1864-Feb-
    ruary 1865)
Hardeman's Brigade, Bee's Division, Wharton's Cavalry Corps, Trans-Missis-
    sippi Department (February-May 1865)
Battles: New Mexico Campaign (January-April 1862)
Valverde (February 21, 1862)
Glorieta Pass (March 28, 1862)
Galveston Island (January 1, 1863)
Fort Bisland (April 12-13, 1863)
Irish Bend (April 14, 1863)
Brashear City (June 23, 1863)
Donaldsonville (June 28, 1863)
Cox's Plantation (July 12-13, 1863)
Stirling's Plantation (September 29, 1863)
Bayou Bourbeau (November 3, 1863)
Red River Campaign (March-May 1864)
Mansfield (April 8, 1864)
Pleasant Hill (April 9, 1864)
Further Reading: Hall, Martin Hardwick, *Sibley's New Mexico Campaign.*

145.   TEXAS 4TH CAVALRY REGIMENT, ARIZONA BRIGADE

Organization: Organized in February 1863. Surrendered by General E. K. Smith, commanding Trans-Mississippi Department, on May 26, 1865. [NOTE: Except for one company serving in the Eastern Sub-district, District of Texas, New Mexico, and Arizona, Trans-Mississippi Department, this regiment was being chased by other Confederate regiments in Cooke County in northern Texas at the war's close. This was due to their depredations against the local inhabitants.]

First Commander: Spruce McC. Baird (Colonel)

Field Officers: Edward Riordan (Major)

Daniel Showalter (Lieutenant Colonel)

Assignments: District of Texas, New Mexico, and Arizona, Trans-Mississippi Department (February 1863)

Hardeman's Brigade, District of Texas, New Mexico, and Arizona, Trans-Mississippi Department (February-June 1863)

Northern Sub-district, District of Texas, New Mexico, and Arizona, Trans-Mississippi Department (June 1863-September 1864)

7th (Slaughter's) Texas Cavalry Brigade, 3rd (Drayton's) Cavalry Division, 3rd Corps, Trans-Mississippi Department (September 1864-April 1865)

146.   TEXAS 4TH CAVALRY REGIMENT, MOUNTED DRAGOONS

See: TEXAS 12TH CAVALRY REGIMENT

147.   TEXAS 4TH CAVALRY REGIMENT, STATE TROOPS

Organization: Organized for six months in late 1863. Mustered out in early 1864.

First Commander: J. B. Johnson (Colonel)

Field Officers: H. W. Cooke (Major)

Samuel A. Easley (Lieutenant Colonel)

Assignments: Rainey's Brigade, Eastern Sub-district, District of Texas, New Mexico, and Arizona, Trans-Mississippi Department (December 1863-January 1864)

Griffin's Brigade, Eastern Sub-district, District of Texas, New Mexico, and Arizona, Trans-Mississippi Department (January 1864)

148.   TEXAS 5TH CAVALRY REGIMENT

Also Known As: 5th Mounted Rifles

Organization: Organized in September 1861. Surrendered by General E. K. Smith, commanding Trans-Mississippi Department, on May 26, 1865.

First Commander: Thomas Green (Colonel)

Field Officers: Samuel A. Lockridge (Major)

Henry C. McNeill (Lieutenant Colonel, Colonel)

Hugh A. McPhaill (Major)

Denman W. Shannon (Major, Lieutenant Colonel)

Assignments: Sibley's Brigade (September-December 1861)

Army of New Mexico (December 1861-December 1862)

Sibley's-Green's Cavalry Brigade, District of Texas, New Mexico, and Arizona, Trans-Mississippi Department (December 1862-January 1863)

Green's Cavalry Brigade, Eastern Sub-district, District of Texas, New Mexico, and Arizona, Trans-Mississippi Department (January 1863)

Green's Cavalry Brigade, District of West Louisiana, Trans-Mississippi Department (March-May 1863)

Green's-Bagby's Brigade, Green's Cavalry Division, Sub-district of Southwestern Louisiana, District of West Louisiana, Trans-Mississippi Department (May-December 1863)

Green's-Bagby's Brigade, Green's Cavalry Division, Eastern Sub-district, District of Texas, New Mexico, and Arizona, Trans-Mississippi Department (December 1863-March 1864)

Green's-Bagby's Brigade, Green's-Wharton's Cavalry Division, District of West Louisiana, Trans-Mississippi Department (March-September 1864)

3rd (Hardeman's) Texas Cavalry Brigade, 1st (Wharton's) Texas Cavalry Division, 2nd Corps, Trans-Mississippi Department (September 1864-February 1865)

Debray's Brigade, Bee's Division, Wharton's Cavalry Corps, Trans-Mississippi Department (February-May 1865)

Battles: New Mexico Campaign (January-April 1862)

Valverde (February 21, 1862)

Glorieta Pass [four companies] (March 28, 1862)

Los Padillas [detachment Company G] (April 13, 1862)

Galveston Island (January 1, 1863)

Fort Bisland (April 12-13, 1863)

Brashear City (June 23, 1863)

Donaldsonville (June 28, 1863)

Cox's Plantation (July 12-13, 1863)

Stirling's Plantation (September 29, 1863)

Bayou Bourbeau (November 3, 1863)

Red River Campaign (March-May 1864)

Mansfield (April 8, 1864)

Pleasant Hill (April 9, 1864)

Further Reading: Hall, Martin Hardwick, *Sibley's New Mexico Campaign.*

149.   TEXAS 5TH CAVALRY REGIMENT, PARTISAN RANGERS

Organization: Organized by the consolidation of the 9th Partisan Rangers Battalion and the 10th Cavalry Battalion in early 1863. Dismounted in March 1865. Surrendered by General E. K. Smith, commanding Trans-Mississippi Department, on May 26, 1865.

First Commander: Leonidas M. Martin (Colonel)

Field Officers: William N. Mayrant (Major)

William M. Weaver (Lieutenant Colonel)

Assignments: Cooper's Brigade, Steele's Division, District of Arkansas, Trans-Mississippi Department (April-October 1863)

Indian Territory, Trans-Mississippi Department (October 1863-July 1864)

District of the Indian Territory, Trans-Mississippi Department (July 1864)

Gano's Brigade, Cooper's (Indian) Division, District of the Indian Territory, Trans-Mississippi Department (September 1864)

5th (Gano's) Texas Cavalry Brigade, 2nd (Maxey's) Texas Cavalry Division, 1st Corps, Trans-Mississippi Department (September 1864-February 1865)

Northern Sub-district, District of Texas, New Mexico, and Arizona, Trans-Mississippi Department (February 1865)

3rd Texas Infantry Brigade, 1st (Forney's) Texas Infantry Division, 1st Corps, Trans-Mississippi Department (February-April 1865)

Robertson's Brigade, Maxey's Division, District of Texas, New Mexico, and Arizona, Trans-Mississippi Department (April-May 1865)

Battles: near Honey Springs (July 17, 1863)

Massard's Prairie, near Fort Smith [detachment] (July 27, 1864)

Cabin Creek (September 19, 1864)

150.   TEXAS 6TH CAVALRY BATTALION

Organization: Organized in the summer of 1862. Dismounted in 1862. Surrendered by General E. K. Smith, commanding Trans-Mississippi Department, on May 26, 1865.

First Commander: Robert S. Gould (Major, Lieutenant Colonel)

Field Officer: William W. Veser (Major)

Assignments: Randal's Brigade, McCulloch's Division, District of Arkansas, Trans-Mississippi Department (September 1862)

Randal's Brigade, McCulloch's Division, 2nd Corps, Trans-Mississippi Department (September 1862-January 1863)

Randal's Brigade, McCulloch's-Walker's Division, District of Arkansas, Trans-Mississippi Department (February-March 1863)

Randal's Brigade, Walker's Division, District of West Louisiana, Trans-Mississippi Department (May 1863-April 1864)

Randal's-Maclay's Brigade, Walker's Division, District of Arkansas, Trans-Mississippi Department (April-May 1864)

Maclay's Brigade, Walker's Division, District of West Louisiana, Trans-Mississippi Department (May-September 1864)

3rd (Maclay's) Texas Brigade, 1st (Forney's) Texas Division, 1st Corps, Trans-Mississippi Department (September 1864-May 1865)

Battles: Red River Campaign (March-May 1864)

Camden Expedition (March-May 1864)

Mansfield (April 8, 1864)

Pleasant Hill (April 9, 1864)

Jenkins' Ferry (April 30, 1864)

151.   TEXAS 6TH CAVALRY REGIMENT

Also Known As: 2nd Cavalry Regiment

Organization: Organized at Dallas on September 6, 1861. Early in the war it was known as the 2nd Cavalry Regiment.   Dismounted in April 1862. Remounted in late October 1862.   Surrendered by Lieutenant General Richard Taylor, commanding the Department of Alabama, Mississippi, and East Louisiana, at Citronelle, Alabama on May 4, 1865.

First Commander: B. Warren Stone (Colonel)

Field Officers: John S. Griffith (Lieutenant Colonel)

Lawrence S. Ross (Lieutenant Colonel, Colonel)

Peter F. Ross (Major, Lieutenant Colonel)

Jack Wharton (Major, Lieutenant Colonel, Colonel)

Robert M. White (Major)

Stephen B. Wilson (Major)

Assignments: Department of Texas (September 1861)

McCulloch's Division, Department #2 (October-December 1861)

McIntosh's Cavalry Brigade, McCulloch's Division, Department #2 (December 1861-January 1862)

McIntosh's Cavalry Brigade, McCulloch's Division, Trans-Mississippi District, Department #2 (January-March 1862)

Roane's-Phifer's Brigade, Jones'-Maury's Division, Army of the West, Department #2 (April-July 1862)

Phifer's Brigade, Maury's Division, Army of West Tennessee, Department #2 (September-October 1862)

Griffith's-Whitfield's Cavalry Brigade, Maury's Division, Price's Corps, Army of West Tennessee, Department of Mississippi and East Louisiana (October-December 1862)

Whitfield's Brigade, 2nd Division, Van Dorn's Cavalry Corps, Department of Mississippi and East Louisiana (January-February 1863)

Whitfield's Brigade, Jackson's Division, Van Dorn's Cavalry Corps, Department of Mississippi and East Louisiana (February 1863)

Whitfield's Brigade, Jackson's Division, Van Dorn's Cavalry Corps, Army of Tennessee (February-May 1863)

Whitfield's Brigade, Jackson's Cavalry Division, Department of the West (June-July 1863)

Whitfield's Brigade, Jackson's Cavalry Division, Department of Mississippi and East Louisiana (July-August 1863)

Whitfield's-Ross' Brigade, Jackson's Division, Lee's Cavalry Corps, Department of Mississippi and East Louisiana (August 1863-January 1864)

Ross' Brigade, Jackson's Division, Lee's Cavalry Corps, Department of Alabama, Mississippi, and East Louisiana (January-May 1864)

Ross' Brigade, Jackson's Cavalry Division, Army of Mississippi (May-July 1864)

Ross' Brigade, Jackson's Cavalry Division, Army of Tennessee (July 1864-February 1865)

Ross' Brigade, Jackson's Division, Forrest's Cavalry Corps, Department of Alabama, Mississippi, and East Louisiana (February-May 1865)

Battles: Chustenahlah (December 26, 1861)

Pea Ridge (March 7-8, 1862)

Corinth Campaign (April-June 1862)

Corinth (October 3-4, 1862)

Oakland [skirmish] (December 3, 1862)

Holly Springs (December 20, 1862)

Davis' Mills (December 21, 1862)

Middleburg (December 24, 1862)

Thompson's Station (March 5, 1863)

Vicksburg Campaign (May-July 1863)

Jackson Siege (July 1863)

Meridian Campaign (February-March 1864)

Marion County (April 19, 1864)

Atlanta Campaign (May-September 1864)

Atlanta Siege (July-September 1864)

Flat Shoals (July 28, 1864)

Franklin-Nashville Campaign (October 1864-January 1865)

Further Reading: Keen, Newton Asbury, *Living and Fighting with the Texas 6th Cavalry.*

152. TEXAS 7TH CAVALRY BATTALION

Also Known As: 7th Infantry Battalion [erroneously]

Organization: Organized with seven companies on December 7, 1861. Increased to a regiment and designated as the 26th Cavalry Regiment on March

17, 1862. This unit does not appear separately in the index to the *Official Records.*

First Commander: Xavier B. Debray (Lieutenant Colonel)

Field Officers: Samuel B. Davis (Major)

John J. Myers (Major)

Assignments: Department of Texas (December 1861-February 1862)

Eastern District of Texas, Department of Texas (February-March 1862)

153. TEXAS 7TH CAVALRY REGIMENT

Organization: Organized by October 4, 1861. Surrendered by General E. K. Smith, commanding Trans-Mississippi Department, on May 26, 1865. Disbanded at Wild Cat Bluff ca. May 27, 1865.

First Commander: William Steele (Colonel)

Field Officers: Arthur P. Bagby (Major, Lieutenant Colonel, Colonel)

Philemon T. Herbert (Lieutenant Colonel, Colonel)

Gustave Hoffman (Major, Lieutenant Colonel)

Powhatan Jordan (Major, Lieutenant Colonel)

John S. Sutton (Lieutenant Colonel)

Assignments: Sibley's Brigade (December 1861)

Army of New Mexico (December 1861-December 1862)

Sibley's-Green's Cavalry Brigade, District of Texas, New Mexico, and Arizona, Trans-Mississippi Department (December 1862-January 1863)

Green's Cavalry Brigade, Eastern Sub-district, District of Texas, New Mexico, and Arizona, Trans-Mississippi Department (January 1863)

Green's Cavalry Brigade, District of West Louisiana, Trans-Mississippi Department (March-May 1863)

Green's-Bagby's Brigade, Green's Cavalry Division, Sub-district of Southwestern Louisiana, District of West Louisiana, Trans-Mississippi Department (May-December 1863)

Green's-Bagby's Brigade, Green's Cavalry Division, Eastern Sub-district, District of Texas, New Mexico, and Arizona, Trans-Mississippi Department (December 1863-March 1864)

Green's-Bagby's Brigade, Green's-Wharton's Cavalry Division, District of West Louisiana, Trans-Mississippi Department (March-September 1864)

3rd (Hardeman's) Texas Cavalry Brigade, 1st (Wharton's) Texas Cavalry Division, 2nd Corps, Trans-Mississippi Department (September 1864-February 1865)

Bagby's Cavalry Brigade, District of West Louisiana, Trans-Mississippi Department (February-April 1865)

Bagby's Cavalry Brigade, District of Arkansas and West Louisiana, Trans-Mississippi Department (April-May 1865)

Battles: New Mexico Campaign (January-April 1862)
Valverde (February 21, 1862)
Glorieta Pass [four companies] (March 28, 1862)
Fort Bisland (April 12-13, 1863)
Brashear City (June 23, 1863)
Donaldsonville (June 28, 1863)
Cox's Plantation (July 12-13, 1863)
Stirling's Plantation (September 29, 1863)
Bayou Bourbeau (November 3, 1863)
Red River Campaign (March-May 1864)
Many (April 2, 1864)
Mansfield (April 8, 1864)
Pleasant Hill (April 9, 1864)
Monett's Ferry (April 23, 1864)
Bayou Cotile [skirmish] (April 25, 1864)
McNutt's Hill (April 26, 1864)
Mansura (May 16, 1864)
Further Reading: Hall, Martin Hardwick, *Sibley's New Mexico Campaign.*

154. TEXAS 8TH CAVALRY BATTALION

Organization: Organized by the reduction of the 1st Mounted Rifles Regiment
to a battalion of five companies ca. April 1862. Consolidated with the 3rd Cavalry
Battalion and designated as the 1st Cavalry Regiment ca. May 1863.
First Commander: Joseph Taylor (Major)
Assignments: Western Sub-district of Texas, Department of Texas (April-
    May 1862)
Western Sub-district of Texas, Trans-Mississippi Department (May-August
    1862)
District of Texas, Trans-Mississippi Department (August-October 1862)
Sub-district of the Rio Grande, District of Texas, Trans-Mississippi Department
    (October-December 1862)
Sub-district of the Rio Grande, District of Texas, New Mexico, and Arizona,
    Trans-Mississippi Department (December 1862-January 1863)
Western Sub-district, District of Texas, New Mexico, and Arizona, Trans-Mis-
    sissippi Department (January 1863)
Battle: Nueces River, near Fort Clark (August 10, 1862)
Further Reading: Spencer, John W., *Terrell's Texas Cavalry.*

155. TEXAS 8TH CAVALRY REGIMENT

Also Known As: 1st Texas Rangers
Terry's Texas Rangers

Organization: Organized for the war at Houston in September 1861. Mustered into Confederate service for the war at Houston on September 9, 1861. Surrendered by General Joseph E. Johnston at Durham Station, Orange County, North Carolina on April 26, 1865.

First Commander: Benjamin F. Terry (Colonel)

Field Officers: Samuel P. Christian (Major, Lieutenant Colonel)

Gustave Cook (Major, Lieutenant Colonel, Colonel)

Marcus L. Evans (Major, Lieutenant Colonel)

Stephen C. Ferrill (Major, Lieutenant Colonel)

Thomas Harrison (Major, Lieutenant Colonel, Colonel)

William R Jarman (Major)

Thomas S. Lubbock (Lieutenant Colonel, Colonel)

Leander M. Rayburn (Major)

John G. Walker (Lieutenant Colonel)

John A. Wharton (Colonel)

Assignments: Department of Texas (September 1861)

Central Geographical Division of Kentucky, Department #2 (September-October 1861)

Reserve, Central Army of Kentucky, Department #2 (October 1861-January 1862)

Hindman's Brigade, Hardee's Division, Central Army of Kentucky, Department #2 (January-February 1862)

Unattached, Central Army of Kentucky, Department #2 (February-March 1862)

Unattached Cavalry, Army of the Mississippi, Department #2 (March-April 1862)

Beall's Cavalry Brigade, Department #2 (April-May 1862)

Forrest's Cavalry Brigade, Army of the Mississippi, Department #2 (June-September 1862)

Wheeler's-Wharton's Cavalry Brigade, Left Wing, Army of the Mississippi, Department #2 (September-November 1862)

Wharton's Cavalry Brigade, 2nd Corps, Army of the Mississippi, Department #2 (November 1862)

Wharton's Cavalry Brigade, 1st Corps, Army of Tennessee (November-December 1862)

Wharton's Brigade, Wheeler's Cavalry Division, Army of Tennessee (December 1862-March 1863)

Wharton's-Harrison's Brigade, Wharton's Division, Wheeler's Cavalry Corps, Army of Tennessee (March-November 1863)

Harrison's Brigade, Wharton's Division, Wheeler's-Martin's Cavalry Corps, Department of East Tennessee (November-December 1863)

Harrison's Brigade, Armstrong's Division, Wheeler's-Martin's Cavalry Corps, Department of East Tennessee (December 1863-February 1864)

Harrison's Brigade, Humes' Division, Wheeler's Cavalry Corps (February-November 1864)

Harrison's Brigade, Humes' Division, Wheeler's Cavalry Corps, Department of South Carolina, Georgia, and Florida (November 1864-February 1865)

Harrison's Brigade, Humes' Division, Wheeler's Cavalry Corps, Hampton's Cavalry Command (February-April 1865)

Hampton's Cavalry Command, Army of Tennessee (April 1865)

Battles: Woodsonville (December 17, 1861)

Shiloh (April 6-7, 1862)

reconnaissance from Shiloh Battlefield (April 8, 1862)

Corinth Campaign (April-June 1862)

Elk River, near Bethel [detachment] (May 9, 1862)

Forrest's Murfreesboro Raid (July 1862)

Capture of Murfreesboro (July 13, 1862)

near Nashville [skirmish] (July 21, 1862)

Perryville (October 8, 1862)

near Nashville [skirmish] (December 23, 1862)

Murfreesboro (December 31, 1862-January 3, 1863)

near Triune [skirmish] (March 21, 1863)

Wheeler's Louisville & Nashville and Nashville & Chattanooga Railroads Raid (April 7-11, 1863)

Tullahoma Campaign (June 1863)

Chickamauga (September 19-20, 1863)

Chattanooga Siege (September-November 1863)

Knoxville Siege (November-December 1863)

Atlanta Campaign (May-September 1864)

Atlanta Siege (July-September 1864)

White River (July 30, 1864)

Brown's Mill (July 30, 1864)

Strawberry Plains (August 24, 1864)

Saltville (October 2, 1864)

Carolinas Campaign (February-April 1865)

Bentonville (March 19-21, 1865)

Further Reading: Giles, Leonidas B., *Terry's Texas Rangers.* Dodd, Ephraim Shelby, *Diary of Ephraim Shelby Dodd, Member of Company D, Terry's Texas Rangers, December 4, 1862-January 1, 1864.*

156.   TEXAS 9TH CAVALRY BATTALION, PARTISAN RANGERS

Organization: Organized in the fall of 1862. Consolidated with the 10th Cavalry Battalion and designated as the 5th Partisan Rangers Regiment in early 1863.

First Commander: John L. Randolph (Major)

Assignments: Cooper's Brigade, District of Arkansas, Trans-Mississippi Department (November-December 1862)

Cooper's Brigade, Roane's Division, 1st Corps, Trans-Mississippi Department (December 1862-January 1863)

157.   TEXAS 9TH CAVALRY REGIMENT

Also Known As: 4th Cavalry Regiment [early in the war]

Organization: Organized for 12 months at Camp Reeves, near Sherman, Grayson County on October 2, 1861. Mustered into Confederate service for one year on October 14, 1861. Dismounted in April 1862. Reorganized on May 26, 1862. Remounted later in 1862. Surrendered by Lieutenant General Richard Taylor, commanding the Department of Alabama, Mississippi, and East Louisiana, at Citronelle, Alabama on May 4, 1865.

First Commander: William B. Sims (Colonel)

Field Officers: James C. Bates (Major)

Thomas G. Berry (Lieutenant Colonel)

H. C. Dial (Major)

J. N. Dodson (Major, Lieutenant Colonel)

Dudley W. Jones (Lieutenant Colonel, Colonel)

William Quayle (Lieutenant Colonel)

Nathan W. Townes (Major, Colonel)

Assignments: Department of Texas (October 1861)

McCulloch's Division, Department #2 (November-December 1861)

McIntosh's Cavalry Brigade, McCulloch's Division, Department #2 (December 1861-January 1862)

McIntosh's Cavalry Brigade, McCulloch's Division, Trans-Mississippi District, Department #2 (January-March 1862)

Roane's-Phifer's Brigade, Jones'-Maury's Division, Army of the West, Department #2 (April-July 1862)

Phifer's Brigade, Maury's Division, Army of West Tennessee, Department #2 (September-October 1862)

Griffith's-Whitfield's Cavalry Brigade, Maury's Division, Price's Corps, Army of West Tennessee, Department of Mississippi and East Louisiana (October-December 1862)

Whitfield's Brigade, 2nd Division, Van Dorn's Cavalry Corps, Department of Mississippi and East Louisiana (January-February 1863)

Whitfield's Brigade, Jackson's Division, Van Dorn's Cavalry Corps, Department of Mississippi and East Louisiana (February 1863)

Whitfield's Brigade, Jackson's Division, Van Dorn's Cavalry Corps, Army of Tennessee (February-May 1863)

Whitfield's Brigade, Jackson's Cavalry Division, Department of the West (June-July 1863)

Whitfield's Brigade, Jackson's Cavalry Division, Department of Mississippi and East Louisiana (July-August 1863)

Whitfield's-Ross' Brigade, Jackson's Division, Lee's Cavalry Corps, Department of Mississippi and East Louisiana (August 1863-January 1864)

Ross' Brigade, Jackson's Division, Lee's Cavalry Corps, Department of Alabama, Mississippi, and East Louisiana (January-May 1864)

Ross' Brigade, Jackson's Cavalry Division, Army of Mississippi (May-July 1864)

Ross' Brigade, Jackson's Cavalry Division, Army of Tennessee (July 1864-February 1865)

Ross' Brigade, Jackson's Division, Forrest's Cavalry Corps, Department of Alabama, Mississippi, and East Louisiana (February-May 1865)

Battles: Round Mountain [detachment] (November 19, 1861)

Chusto-Talash (Decmeber 9, 1861)

Pea Ridge (March 7-8, 1862)

Corinth Campaign (April-June 1862)

Farmington (May 9, 1862)

Iuka (September 19, 1862)

Corinth (October 3-4, 1862)

Hatchie Bridge (October 7, 1862)

Holly Springs (December 20, 1862)

Davis' Mills (December 21, 1862)

Middleburg (December 24, 1862)

Thompson's Station (March 5, 1863)

Vicksburg Campaign (May-July 1863)

Mechanicsburg (June 4, 1863)

Jackson Siege (July 1863)

Meridian Campaign (February-March 1864)

Snyder's Bluff (March 30, 1864)

Roach Plantation (March 31, 1864)

Marion County (April 19, 1864)

Atlanta Campaign (May-September 1864)

New Hope Church (May 25-27, 1864)

Marietta (June 27-July 26, 1864)

Flat Shoals (July 28, 1864)

Lovejoy's Station (July 29, 1864)

Newnan (July 30, 1864)
Atlanta Siege (July-September 1864)
Fairburn (August 16, 1864)
Jonesboro (August 31-September 1, 1864)
Franklin-Nashville Campaign (October 1864-January 1865)
Campbellsville (November 24, 1864)
Franklin (November 30, 1864)
Murfreesboro (December 15, 1864)
Nashville (December 15-16, 1864)
Further Reading: Kerr, Homer L., ed., *Fighting With Ross' Texas Cavalry Brigade C.S.A.: The Diary of George L. Griscom, Adjutant, 9th Texas Cavalry Regiment.*

158. TEXAS 10TH CAVALRY BATTALION

Organization: Organized in late 1862. Consolidated with the 9th Partisan Rangers Battalion and designated as the 5th Partisan Rangers Regiment in early 1863.
First Commander: Leonidas M. Martin (Major)

159. TEXAS 10TH CAVALRY REGIMENT

Organization: Organized in the fall of 1861. Dismounted in April 1862. Surrendered by Lieutenant General Richard Taylor, commanding the Department of Alabama, Mississippi, and East Louisiana, at Citronelle, Alabama on May 4, 1865.
First Commander: Matthew F. Locke (Colonel)
Field Officers: James M. Barton (Lieutenant Colonel)
William de la F. Craig (Major, Lieutenant Colonel)
C. R. Earp (Lieutenant Colonel, Colonel)
Wiley B. Ector (Major)
Hullum D. E. Redwine (Major)
Assignments: Department of Texas (October 1861-February 1862)
Trans-Mississippi District, Department #2 (April 1862)
Hogg's-Cabell's Brigade, McCown's Division, Army of the West, Department #2 (April-July 1862)
Ector's Brigade, McCown's Division, Department of East Tennessee (July-August 1862)
Ector's Brigade, McCown's Division, Army of Kentucky, Department #2 (August-October 1862)
Ector's Brigade, McCown's Division, Department of East Tennessee (October-November 1862)

Ector's Brigade, McCown's Division, 3rd (E. K. Smith's) Corps, Army of Tennessee (November 1862-March 1863)

Ector's Brigade, McCown's Division, 1st Corps, Army of Tennessee (March-May 1863)

Ector's Brigade, Walker's Division, Department of the West (June-July 1863)

Ector's Brigade, Walker's Division, Department of Mississippi and East Louisiana (July-August 1863)

Ector's Brigade, Walker's Division, Reserve Corps, Army of Tennessee (August-September 1863)

Ector's Brigade, French's Division, Department of Mississippi and East Louisiana (October 1863-January 1864)

Ector's Brigade, French's Division, Department of Alabama, Mississippi, and East Louisiana (January-May 1864)

Ector's Brigade, French's Division, Army of Mississippi (May-July 1864)

Ector's Brigade, French's Division, 3rd Corps, Army of Tennessee (July 1864-January 1865)

Ector's Brigade, French's Division, District of the Gulf, Department of Alabama, Mississippi, and East Louisiana (February-April 1865)

Ector's Brigade, French's Division, Department of Alabama, Mississippi, and East Louisiana (April 1865)

Battles: Corinth Campaign (April-June 1862)

Kentucky Campaign (August-October 1862)

Richmond (August 30, 1862)

Murfreesboro (December 31, 1862-January 3, 1863)

Vicksburg Campaign (May-July 1863)

Jackson (May 14, 1863)

Jackson Siege (July 1863)

Chickamauga (September 19-20, 1863)

Meridian Campaign (February-March 1864)

Atlanta Campaign (May-September 1864)

Cassville (May 19-22, 1864)

Kennesaw Mountain (June 27, 1864)

Atlanta (July 22, 1864)

Atlanta Siege (July-September 1864)

Jonesboro (August 31-September 1, 1864)

Lovejoy's Station (September 2, 1864)

Allatoona (October 5, 1864)

Franklin (November 30, 1864)

Nashville (December 15-16, 1864)

Mobile (March 17-April 12, 1865)

Fort Blakely (April 1-9, 1865)

160. TEXAS 11TH CAVALRY AND INFANTRY BATTALION

Organization: Organized by the reorganization of the 6th Infantry Battalion in April 1862. Consolidated with the 21st Infantry Battalion and designated as the 21st Infantry Regiment in November 1864.

First Commander: Ashley W. Spaight (Lieutenant Colonel)

Field Officer: J. S. Irvine (Major)

Assignments: Eastern District, Department of Texas (April-May 1862)

Eastern District of Texas, Trans-Mississippi Department (May-August 1862)

Eastern District, District of Texas, Trans-Mississippi Department (August-December 1862)

District of Texas, New Mexico, and Arizona, Trans-Mississippi Department (December 1862-January 1863)

Eastern Sub-district, District of Texas, New Mexico, and Arizona, Trans-Mississippi Department (February 1863-September 1864)

6th (Hébert's) Texas Brigade, 2nd (Hébert's) Texas Division 3rd Corps, Trans-Mississippi Department (September-November 1864)

Battles: Sabine Pass (September 23-25, 1862)

Taylor's Bayou (September 27, 1862)

Sabine Pass [Company A] (October 29, 1862)

Attack on Blockading Squadron at Sabine Pass [volunteer detachment] (January 21, 1863)

Sabine Pass [detachment] (September 8, 1863)

Calcasieu Pass (May 6, 1864)

161. TEXAS 11TH CAVALRY REGIMENT

Also Known As: 3rd Cavalry Regiment [early in the war]

Organization: Organized in the summer of 1861. Dismounted in 1862. Remounted in 1863. Surrendered by General Joseph E. Johnston at Durham Station, Orange County, North Carolina on April 26, 1865.

First Commander: William C. Young (Colonel)

Field Officers: Henry F. Bone (Major)

Joseph M. Bounds (Lieutenant Colonel, Colonel)

John C. Burks (Colonel)

James J. Diamond (Lieutenant Colonel, Colonel)

Robert W. Hooks (Lieutenant Colonel, Colonel)

John W. Mayrant (Major)

Otis M. Messick (Major, Lieutenant Colonel, Colonel)

Andrew J. Nicholson (Lieutenant Colonel)

John B. Puryear (Major)

George R. Reeves (Colonel)

Assignments: Department of Texas (July-November 1861)

McCulloch's Division, Department #2 (December 1861)

Hébert's Brigade, McCulloch's Division, Department #2 (December 1861-January 1862)

Hébert's Brigade, McCulloch's Division, Trans-Mississippi District, Department #2 (January-February 1862)

McIntosh's Cavalry Brigade, McCulloch's Division, Trans-Mississippi District, Department #2 (February-March 1862)

Greer's Cavalry Brigade, Price's Division, Trans-Mississippi District, Department #2 (March-April 1862)

Hogg's-Cabell's Brigade, McCown's Division, Army of the West, Department #2 (April-July 1862)

Ector's Brigade, McCown's Division, Department of East Tennessee (July-August 1862)

Ector's Brigade, McCown's Division, Army of Kentucky, Department #2 (August-October 1862)

Ector's Brigade, McCown's Division, Department of East Tennessee (October-November 1862)

Ector's Brigade, McCown's Division, 3rd (E. K. Smith's) Corps, Army of Tennessee (November 1862-January 1863)

Wharton's Brigade, Wheeler's Cavalry Division, Army of Tennessee (January-March 1863)

Wharton's-Harrison's Brigade, Wharton's Division, Wheeler's Cavalry Corps, Army of Tennessee (March-November 1863)

Harrison's Brigade, Wharton's Division, Wheeler's-Martin's Cavalry Corps, Department of East Tennessee (November-December 1863)

Harrison's Brigade, Armstrong's Division, Wheeler's-Martin's Cavalry Corps, Department of East Tennessee (December 1863-February 1864)

Harrison's Brigade, Humes' Division, Wheeler's Cavalry Corps (February-November 1864)

Harrison's Brigade, Humes' Division, Wheeler's Cavalry Corps, Department of South Carolina, Georgia, and Florida (November 1864-February 1865)

Harrison's Brigade, Humes' Division, Wheeler's Cavalry Corps, Hampton's Cavalry Command (February-April 1865)

Hampton's Cavalry Command, Army of Tennessee (April 1865)

Battles: Chustenahlah [seven companies] (December 26, 1861)

Pea Ridge (March 7-8, 1862)

Corinth Campaign (April-June 1862)

Richmond (August 30, 1862)

Murfreesboro (December 31, 1862-January 3, 1863)

Wheeler's Louisville & Nashville and Nashville & Chattanooga Railroads Raid (April 7-11, 1863)

Tullahoma Campaign (June 1863)
Chickamauga (September 19-20, 1863)
Chattanooga Siege (September-November 1863)
Knoxville Siege (November-December 1863)
Atlanta Campaign (May-September 1864)
Atlanta Siege (July-September 1864)
Flat Shoals (July 28, 1864)
Strawberry Plains (August 24, 1864)
Saltville (October 2, 1864)
Savannah Campaign (November-December 1864)
Carolinas Campaign (February-April 1865)

162. TEXAS 12TH CAVALRY BATTALION

Organization: Organized by the assignment of companies from the 13th Infantry Regiment in mid-1862. Consolidated with Rountree's Cavalry Battalion and designated as the 35th (Brown's) Cavalry Regiment in mid-1863.
First Commander: Reuben R. Brown (Lieutenant Colonel)
Field Officer: Samuel W. Perkins (Major)
Assignments: Sub-district of Houston, Trans-Mississippi Department (July-August 1862)
Sub-district of Houston, District of Texas, Trans-Mississippi Department (August-December 1862)
District of Texas, New Mexico, and Arizona, Trans-Mississippi Department (December 1862-May 1863)
Battle: near Matagorda [detachment] (November 20, 1862)

163. TEXAS 12TH CAVALRY REGIMENT

Also Known As: 4th Texas Mounted Dragoons
Organization: Organized for 12 months at Rocket Springs, near Waxahachie on September 11, 1861. Mustered into Confederate service at Camp Hébert, near Hempstead on October 28, 1861. Reorganized for the war on May 24, 1862. Surrendered by General E. K. Smith, commanding Trans-Mississippi Department, on May 26, 1865.
First Commander: William H. Parsons (Colonel)
Field Officers: Andrew B. Burleson (Lieutenant Colonel)
Lochlin Johnson Farrar (Major)
John W. Mullen (Lieutenant Colonel)
E. W. Rogers (Major)
Assignments: Department of Texas (September 1861-February 1862)
Eastern District of Texas, Department of Texas (February-March 1862)

Rust's-Parsons' Cavalry Brigade, Trans-Mississippi District, Department #2 (March-May 1862)

Trans-Mississippi Department (May-June 1862)

W. H. Parsons' Cavalry Brigade, Unattached, Trans-Mississippi Department (July-August 1862)

W. H. Parsons' Cavalry Brigade, Unattached, District of Arkansas, Trans-Mississippi Department (August-September 1862)

W. H. Parsons' Cavalry Brigade, 2nd Corps, Army of the West, Trans-Mississippi Department (September-October 1862)

Hawes' Brigade, Churchill's Division, 2nd Corps, Army of the West, Trans-Mississippi Department (December 1862-January 1863)

Unattached, Frost's Division, District of Arkansas, Trans-Mississippi Department (April-June 1863)

Unassigned, District of West Louisiana, Trans-Mississippi Department (June-July 1863)

Carter's Brigade, Walker's Division, District of Arkansas, Trans-Mississippi Department (July-September 1863)

Carter's-Parsons' Cavalry Brigade, District of Arkansas, Trans-Mississippi Department (September 1863-March 1864)

Carter's-Parson's Brigade, Steele's Cavalry Division, District of West Louisiana, Trans-Mississippi Department (March-September 1864)

1st (Steele's) Texas Cavalry Brigade, 1st (Wharton's) Cavalry Division, 2nd Corps, Trans-Mississippi Department (September 1864-February 1865)

Parsons' Brigade, Steele's Division, Wharton's Cavalry Corps, Trans-Mississippi Department (February-May 1865)

Battles: near Searcy [3 companies] (May 19, 1862)

Round Hill, on Cache River (July 7, 1862)

Hughes' Ferry, L'Anguille River (August 3, 1862)

Little Rock Campaign (August-September 1863)

Red River Campaign (March-May 1864)

Further Reading: Bailey, Anne J., *Between the Enemy and Texas: Parson's Texas Cavalry in the Civil War*. Gallaway, B. P., *The Ragged Rebel: A Common Soldier in W. H. Parsons' Texas Cavalry, 1861-1865*.

164. TEXAS 13TH CAVALRY BATTALION

Organization: Organized in the summer of 1862. Surrendered by General E. K. Smith, commanding Trans-Mississippi Department, on May 26, 1865.

First Commander: Edward Waller, Jr. (Major, Lieutenant Colonel)

Field Officer: Hannibal H. Boone (Major)

Assignments: Unattached, District of West Louisiana, Trans-Mississippi Department (August 1862-May 1863)

Unattached, Sub-district of Southwestern Louisiana, District of West Louisiana, Trans-Mississippi Department (September 1863)

Green's-Bagby's Brigade, Green's Cavalry Division, Eastern Sub-district, District of Texas, New Mexico, and Arizona, Trans-Mississippi Department (December 1863-March 1864)

Green's-Bagby's Brigade, Green's-Wharton's Cavalry Division, District of West Louisiana, Trans-Mississippi Department (March-September 1864)

3rd (Hardeman's) Texas Cavalry Brigade, 1st (Wharton's) Texas Cavalry Division, 2nd Corps, Trans-Mississippi Department (September 1864-February 1865)

Lane's Brigade, Steele's Division, Wharton's Cavalry Corps, Trans-Mississippi Department (February-May 1865)

Battles: Fort Bisland (April 12-13, 1863)

Brashear City (June 23, 1863)

Donaldsonville (June 28, 1863)

Stirling's Plantation (September 29, 1863)

Bayou Bourbeau (November 3, 1863)

Red River Campaign (March-May 1864)

Mansfield (April 8, 1864)

Pleasant Hill (April 9, 1864)

165. TEXAS 13TH CAVALRY REGIMENT

Organization: Organized in early 1862. Dismounted in 1862. Surrendered by General E. K. Smith, commanding Trans-Mississippi Department, on May 26, 1865.

First Commander: John H. Burnett (Colonel)

Field Officers: Charles R. Beaty (Major, Lieutenant Colonel)

Anderson F. Crawford (Lieutenant Colonel, Colonel)

Elias T. Seale (Major)

Assignments: Eastern District of Texas, Department of Texas (February-May 1862)

Eastern District of Texas, Trans-Mississippi Department (May-August 1862)

Young's Brigade, McCulloch's Division, 2nd Corps, Trans-Mississippi Department (September 1862-January 1863)

Young's-Hawes' Brigade, McCulloch's-Walker's Division, District of Arkansas, Trans-Mississippi Department (February-March 1863)

Hawes'-Waul's Brigade, Walker's Division, District of West Louisiana, Trans-Mississippi Department (May 1863-April 1864)

Waul's Brigade, Walker's Division, District of Arkansas, Trans-Mississippi Department (April-May 1864)

Waul's Brigade, Walker's Division, District of Arkansas, Trans-Mississippi
    Department (May-September 1864)
1st (Waul's) Texas Brigade, 1st (Forney's) Texas Division, 1st Corps, Trans-
    Mississippi Department (September 1864-May 1865)
Battles: Young's Point (June 9, 1863)
Red River Campaign (March-May 1864)
Camden Expedition (March-May 1864)
Mansfield (April 8, 1864)
Pleasant Hill (April 9, 1864)
Jenkins' Ferry (April 30, 1864)

166. TEXAS 14TH CAVALRY BATTALION

Organization: Organized with two companies in early 1862. Increased to a
regiment and designated as the 33rd Cavalry Regiment in the spring of 1863.
First Commander: James Duff (Captain, Major, Lieutenant Colonel)
Field Officer: James R. Sweet (Major)
Assignments: Sub-district of the Rio Grande, Western District of Texas,
    Department of Texas (April-May 1862)
Sub-district of the Rio Grande, Western District of Texas, Trans-Mississippi
    Department (May-August 1862)
Sub-district of the Rio Grande, District of Texas, Trans-Mississippi Department
    (August-December 1862)
Sub-district of the Rio Grande, District of Texas, New Mexico, and Arizona,
    Trans-Mississippi Department (December 1862-January 1863)
Western Sub-district, District of Texas, New Mexico, and Arizona, Trans-Mis-
    sissippi Department (January-March 1863)

167. TEXAS 14TH CAVALRY REGIMENT

Organization: Organized in the summer of 1861. Mustered into Confederate
service at Dallas in September 1861. Dismounted at Little Rock, Arkansas in
March or April 1862. Reorganized in May 1862. Surrendered by Lieutenant
General Richard Taylor, commanding the Department of Alabama, Missis-
sippi, and East Louisiana, at Citronelle, Alabama on May 4, 1865.
First Commander: Middleton T. Johnson (Colonel)
Field Officers: John L. Camp (Colonel)
Thompson Camp (Major)
Matthew D. Ector (Colonel)
Fleming H. Garrison (Major)
Abraham Harris (Lieutenant Colonel)
Samuel F. Mains (Lieutenant Colonel)
Lem. Purdy (Major)

Assignments: Department of Texas (September 1861-February 1862)

Rust's-Parsons' Cavalry Brigade, Trans-Mississippi District, Department #2 (March-April 1862)

Hogg's-Cabell's Brigade, McCown's Division, Army of the West, Department #2 (April-July 1862)

Ector's Brigade, McCown's Division, Department of East Tennessee (July-August 1862)

Ector's Brigade, McCown's Division, Army of Kentucky, Department #2 (August-October 1862)

Ector's Brigade, McCown's Division, Department of East Tennessee (October-November 1862)

Ector's Brigade, McCown's Division, 3rd (E. K. Smith's) Corps, Army of Tennessee (November 1862-March 1863)

Ector's Brigade, McCown's Division, 1st Corps, Army of Tennessee (March-May 1863)

Ector's Brigade, Walker's Division, Department of the West (June-July 1863)

Ector's Brigade, Walker's Division, Department of Mississippi and East Louisiana (July-August 1863)

Ector's Brigade, Walker's Division, Reserve Corps, Army of Tennessee (August-September 1863)

Ector's Brigade, French's Division, Department of Mississippi and East Louisiana (October 1863-January 1864)

Ector's Brigade, French's Division, Department of Alabama, Mississippi, and East Louisiana (January-May 1864)

Ector's Brigade, French's Division, Army of Mississippi (May-July 1864)

Ector's Brigade, French's Division, 3rd Corps, Army of Tennessee (July 1864-January 1865)

Ector's Brigade, French's Division, District of the Gulf, Department of Alabama, Mississippi, and East Louisiana (February-April 1865)

Ector's Brigade, French's Division, Department of Alabama, Mississippi, and East Louisiana (April 1865)

Battles: Corinth Campaign (April-June 1862)

Kentucky Campaign (August-October 1862)

Richmond (August 30, 1862)

Murfreesboro (December 31, 1862-January 3, 1863)

Vicksburg Campaign (May-July 1863)

Jackson (May 14, 1863)

Jackson Siege (July 1863)

Chickamauga (September 19-20, 1863)

Meridian Campaign (February-March 1864)

Atlanta Campaign (May-September 1864)

Cassville (May 19-22, 1864)
Kennesaw Mountain (June 27, 1864)
Peach Tree Creek (July 20, 1864)
Atlanta (July 22, 1864)
Atlanta Siege (July-September 1864)
Jonesboro (August 31-September 1, 1864)
Lovejoy's Station (September 2, 1864)
Allatoona (October 5, 1864)
Franklin (November 30, 1864)
Nashville (December 15-16, 1864)
Mobile (March 17-April 12, 1865)
Fort Blakely (April 1-9, 1865)

168. TEXAS 15TH CAVALRY BATTALION, STATE TROOPS

Organization: Organized 1863. This battalion appears only once in the *Official Records* as being overdue in reporting to the Northern Sub-district, District of Texas, New Mexico, and Arizona, Trans-Mississippi Department in October 1863.

169. TEXAS 15TH CAVALRY REGIMENT

Also Known As: 32nd Cavalry Regiment
Organization: Organized at McKinney in early 1862. Dismounted in April 1862. Surrendered at Arkansas Post on January 11, 1863. Exchanged in April 1863. Field consolidation with the 6th and 10th Infantry Regiments from July 1863 to April 9, 1865. The 10th Infantry Regiment was detached from this field consolidation between January and April 1864. Consolidated with the 6th, 7th, and 10th Infantry Regiments and the 17th, 18th, 24th, and 25th Cavalry Regiments [dismounted] and designated as the 1st Infantry Regiment Consolidated at Smithfield, North Carolina on April 9, 1865.
First Commander: George H. Sweet (Colonel)
Field Officers: William H. Cathey (Major)
William K. Masten (Lieutenant Colonel)
George B. Pickett (Major, Lieutenant Colonel)
Valerius P. Sanders (Major)
Assignments: Rust's-Parsons' Cavalry Brigade, Trans-Mississippi District, Department #2 (March-May 1862)
Trans-Mississippi Department (June-August 1862)
District of Arkansas, Trans-Mississippi Department (August-September 1862)
Sweet's Brigade, Nelson's Division, District of Arkansas, Trans-Mississippi Department (September 1862)

Nelson's-Deshler's Brigade, Nelson's-Churchill's Division, 2nd Corps, Trans-Mississippi Department (September-December 1862)

Deshler's Brigade, Chruchill's Division, District of Arkansas, Trans-Mississippi Department (December 1862-January 1863)

Chruchill's-Deshler's-Smith's Brigade, Cleburne's Division, 2nd Corps, Army of Tennessee (July-November 1863)

Smith's-Granbury's Brigade, Cleburne's Division, 1st Corps, Army of Tennessee (November 1863-April 1865)

Battles: Arkansas Post (January 4-11, 1863)
Chickamauga (September 19-20, 1863)
Chattanooga Siege (September-November 1863)
Chattanooga (November 23-25, 1863)
Atlanta Campaign (May-September 1864)
Pickett's Mill (May 27, 1864)
New Hope Church (June 27, 1864)
Atlanta Siege (July-September 1864)
Jonesboro (August 31-September 1, 1864)
Franklin (November 30, 1864)
Nashville (December 15-16, 1864)
Carolinas Campaign (February-April 1865)
Bentonville (March 19-21, 1865)

170. TEXAS 15TH (ANDREWS') CAVALRY REGIMENT

See: TEXAS 32ND CAVALRY REGIMENT

171. TEXAS 16TH CAVALRY REGIMENT

Organization: Organized at Dallas in early 1862. Dismounted in April 1862. Surrendered by General E. K. Smith, commanding Trans-Mississippi Department, on May 26, 1865.

First Commander: William Fitzhugh (Colonel)

Field Officers: William W. Diamond (Major, Lieutenant Colonel)
Edward P. Gregg (Lieutenant Colonel, Colonel)

Assignments: Department of Texas (January-February 1862)
Eastern District of Texas, Department of Texas (February-May 1862)
Eastern District of Texas, Trans-Mississippi Department (May-August 1862)
Flournoy's Brigade, Nelson's-McCulloch's Division, 2nd Corps, Trans-Mississippi Department (September 1862-January 1863)
Flournoy's Brigade, McCulloch's-Walker's Division, District of Arkansas, Trans-Mississippi Department (February-March 1863)
McCulloch's-Flournoy's-Scurry's Brigade, Walker's Division, District of West Louisiana, Trans-Mississippi Department (May 1863-April 1864)

Scurry's-Waterhouse's Brigade, Walker's Division, District of Arkansas, Trans-
   Mississippi Department (April-May 1864)
Waterhouse's Brigade, Walker's Division, District of West Louisiana, Trans-
   Mississippi Department (May-September 1864)
2nd (Waterhouse's) Texas Brigade, 1st (Forney's) Texas Division, 1st Corps,
   Trans-Mississippi Department (September 1864-May 1865)
Battles: Round Hill, on Cache River (July 7, 1862)
Milliken's Bend (June 7, 1863)
Red River Campaign (March-May 1864)
Camden Expedition (March-May 1864)
Mansfield (April 8, 1864)
Pleasant Hill (April 9, 1864)
Jenkins' Ferry (April 30, 1864)

172.   TEXAS 17TH CAVALRY BATTALION, STATE TROOPS

Organization: Organized in mid-1863. This battalion appears only once in
the *Official Records* as being ordered back from the line of the Sabine River in
October 1863.
Assignment: Eastern Sub-district, District of Texas, New Mexico, and Arizona, Trans-Mississippi Department (October 1863)

173.   TEXAS 17TH CAVALRY REGIMENT

Organization: Organized in early 1862. Dismounted in April 1862. Surren-
dered at Arkansas Post on January 11, 1863. Exchanged in April 1863. Field
consolidation with the 18th Cavalry Regiment from July 1863 to April 9, 1865.
Additional field consolidation with the 24th and 25th Cavalry Regiments from
July 1864 to April 9, 1865. Consolidated with the 6th, 7th, and 10th Infantry
Regiments and the 15th, 18th, 24th, and 25th Cavalry Regiments (dis-
mounted) and designated as the 1st Infantry Regiment Consolidated at
Smithfield, North Carolina on April 9, 1865.
First Commander: George F. Moore (Colonel)
Field Officers: Sterling B. Hendricks (Lieutenant Colonel)
John McClarty (Major)
Sebron M. Noble (Major, Lieutenant Colonel)
James R. Taylor (Colonel)
Thomas F. Tucker (Major, Colonel)
Assignments: Eastern District of Texas, Department of Texas (March 1862)
Rust's-Parsons' Cavalry Brigade, Trans-Mississippi District, Department #2
   (March-April 1862)
3rd Brigade, McCown's Division, Army of the West, Department #2 (April-
   June 1862)

Trans-Mississippi Department (June-August 1862)

District of Arkansas, Trans-Mississippi Department (August-September 1862)

Sweet's Brigade, Nelson's Division, District of Arkansas, Trans-Mississippi Department (September 1862)

Nelson's-Deshler's Brigade, Nelson's-Churchill's Division, 2nd Corps, Trans-Mississippi Department (September-December 1862)

Deshler's Brigade, Churchill's Division, District of Arkansas, Trans-Mississippi Department (December 1862-January 1863)

Churchill's-Deshler's-Smith's Brigade, Cleburne's Division, 2nd Corps, Army of Tennessee (May-November 1863)

Smith's-Granbury's Brigade, Cleburne's Division, 1st Corps, Army of Tennessee (November 1863-April 1865)

Battles: Corinth Campaign (April-June 1862)

Round Hill, on Cache River (July 7, 1862)

Arkansas Post (January 4-11, 1863)

Fayetteville [detachment] (April 18, 1863)

Chickamauga (September 19-20, 1863)

Chattanooga Siege (September-November 1863)

Chattanooga (November 23-25, 1863)

Atlanta Campaign (May-September 1864)

Pickett's Mill (May 27, 1864)

New Hope Church (June 27, 1864)

Atlanta Siege (July-September 1864)

Jonesboro (August 31-September 1, 1864)

Franklin (November 30, 1864)

Nashville (December 15-16, 1864)

Carolinas Campaign (February-April 1865)

Bentonville (March 19-21, 1865)

174. TEXAS 18TH CAVALRY BATTALION, STATE TROOPS

Organization: Organized in mid-1863. This battalion appears only once in the *Official Records* as being ordered back from the line of the Sabine River in October 1863.

Assignment: Eastern Sub-district, District of Texas, New Mexico, and Arizona, Trans-Mississippi Department (October 1863)

175. TEXAS 18TH CAVALRY REGIMENT

Organization: Organized at Dallas in early 1862. Dismounted in ca. April 1862. Surrendered at Arkansas Post on January 11, 1863. Exchanged in April 1863. Field consolidation with the 17th Cavalry Regiment from July 1863 to April 9, 1865. Additional field consolidation with the 24th and 25th Cavalry

Regiments from July 1864 to April 9, 1865. Consolidated with the 6th, 7th, and 10th, Infantry Regiments and the 15th, 17th, 24th, and 25th Cavalry Regiments (dismounted) and designated as the 1st Infantry Regiment Consolidated at Smithfield, North Carolina on April 9, 1865.

First Commander: Nicholas H. Darnell (Colonel)
Field Officers: John T. Coit (Lieutenant Colonel)
Charles C. Morgan (Major)
William A. Ryan (Major)
Assignments: Trans-Mississippi Department (June-August 1862)
District of Arkansas, Trans-Mississippi Department (August-September 1862)
Sweet's Brigade, Nelson's Division, District of Arkansas, Trans-Mississippi Department (September 1862)
Nelson's-Deshler's Brigade, Nelson's-Churchill's Division, 2nd Corps, Trans-Mississippi Department (September-December 1862)
Deshler's Brigade, Chruchill's Division, District of Arkansas, Trans-Mississippi Department (December 1862-January 1863)
Chruchill's-Deshler's-Smith's Brigade, Cleburne's Division, 2nd Corps, Army of Tennessee (May-November 1863)
Smith's-Granbury's Brigade, Cleburne's Division, 1st Corps, Army of Tennessee (November 1863-April 1865)
Battles: Arkansas Post (January 4-11, 1863)
Chickamauga (September 19-20, 1863)
Chattanooga Siege (September-November 1863)
Chattanooga (November 23-25, 1863)
Atlanta Campaign (May-September 1864)
Pickett's Mill (May 27, 1864)
New Hope Church (June 27, 1864)
Bald Hill (July 21, 1864)
Atlanta Siege (July-September 1864)
Jonesboro (August 31-September 1, 1864)
Franklin (November 30, 1864)
Nashville (December 15-16, 1864)
Carolinas Campaign (February-April 1865)
Bentonville (March 19-21, 1865)

176. TEXAS 19TH CAVALRY REGIMENT

Organization: Organized in mid-1862. Surrendered by General E. K. Smith, commanding Trans-Mississippi Department, on May 26, 1865.
First Commander: Nathaniel M. Burford (Colonel)
Field Officers: Joel T. Daves (Major)
Benjamin W. Watson (Lieutenant Colonel)

Assignments: Eastern District of Texas, Trans-Mississippi Department (July-August 1862)

Unattached, District of Arkansas, Trans-Mississippi Department (August-October 1862)

Hawes' Brigade, Churchill's Division, 2nd Corps, Army of the West, Trans-Mississippi Department (December 1862-January 1863)

Carter's Brigade, Marmaduke's Cavalry Division, District of Arkansas, Trans-Mississippi Department (April-July 1863)

Carter's Cavalry Brigade, Walker's Cavalry Division, District of Arkansas, Trans-Mississippi Department (July-October 1863)

Carter's-Parsons' Cavalry Brigade, District of Arkansas, Trans-Mississippi Department (October 1863-March 1864)

Carter's-Parson's Brigade, Steele's Cavalry Division, District of West Louisiana, Trans-Mississippi Department (March-September 1864)

1st (Steele's) Texas Cavalry Brigade, 1st (Wharton's) Cavalry Division, 2nd Corps, Trans-Mississippi Department (September 1864-February 1865)

Parsons' Brigade, Steele's Division, Wharton's Cavalry Corps, Trans-Mississippi Department (February-May 1865)

Battles: Little Rock Campaign (August-September 1863)

Red River Campaign (March-May 1864)

Mansfield (April 8, 1864)

Pleasant Hill (April 9, 1864)

Blair's Landing (April 12-13, 1864)

Monett's Ferry (April 23, 1864)

Further Reading: Bailey, Anne J., *Between the Enemy and Texas: Parson's Texas Cavalry in the Civil War.*

177. TEXAS 20TH CAVALRY REGIMENT

Organization: Organized in the summer of 1862. Dismounted in 1862. Surrendered by General E. K. Smith, commanding Trans-Mississippi Department, on May 26, 1865.

First Commander: Thomas C. Bass (Colonel)

Field Officers: Dempsey W. Broughton (Major)

Andrew J. Fowler (Lieutenant Colonel)

John R. Johnson (Major)

Thomas D. Taliaferro (Lieutenant Colonel)

Assignments: Cooper's Brigade, Roane's Division, 1st Corps, Army of the West, Trans-Mississippi Department (September-December 1862)

Bradfute's Brigade, Roane's Division, 1st Corps, Army of the West, Trans-Mississippi Department (December 1862-January 1863)

Cabell's Brigade, Steele's Division, District of Arkansas, Trans-Mississippi Department (April-June 1863)

Cooper's Brigade, Steele's Division, District of Arkansas, Trans-Mississippi Department (June-December 1863)

Unattached, District of the Indian Territory, Trans-Mississippi Department (December 1863-September 1864)

Unattached, Cooper's (Indian) Division, Cavalry Corps, Trans-Mississippi Department (September 1864-February 1865)

Bee's Brigade, Maxey's Division, District of Texas, New Mexico, and Arizona, Trans-Mississippi Department (April-May 1865)

Battle: near Honey Springs (July 17, 1863)

178. TEXAS 21ST CAVALRY REGIMENT

Nickname: 1st Texas Lancers

Organization: Organized in early 1862. The 24th and 25th Texas Cavalry Regiments were organized from this regiment at Hempstead on April 24, 1862. Surrendered by General E. K. Smith, commanding Trans-Mississippi Department, on May 26, 1865.

First Commander: George W. Carter (Colonel)

Field Officers: Benjamin D. Chenoweth (Major)

DeWitt C. Giddings (Lieutenant Colonel)

Robert Neyland (Lieutenant Colonel)

William M. Walton (Major)

Assignments: Eastern District, Department of Texas (April 1862)

Carter's Cavalry Brigade, Eastern District, Department of Texas (April-May 1862)

Carter's Cavalry Brigade, Eastern District of Texas, Trans-Mississippi Department (May-August 1862)

Carter's Cavalry Brigade, District of Arkansas, Trans-Mississippi Department (August-September 1862)

Parsons' Cavalry Brigade, 1st Corps, Trans-Mississippi Department (September-October 1862)

Hawes' Brigade, Churchill's Division, 2nd Corps, Army of the West, Trans-Mississippi Department (December 1862-January 1863)

Carter's Brigade, Marmaduke's Cavalry Division, District of Arkansas, Trans-Mississippi Department (April-July 1863)

Carter's Cavalry Brigade, Walker's Cavalry Division, District of Arkansas, Trans-Mississippi Department (July-September 1863)

Carter's-Parsons' Cavalry Brigade, District of Arkansas, Trans-Mississippi Department (September 1863-March 1864)

Carter's-Parson's Brigade, Steele's Cavalry Division, District of West Louisiana,
    Trans-Mississippi Department (March-September 1864)
1st (Steele's) Texas Cavalry Brigade, 1st (Wharton's) Cavalry Division, 2nd
    Corps, Trans-Mississippi Department (September 1864-February 1865)
Lane's Brigade, Steele's Division, Wharton's Cavalry Corps, Trans-Mississippi
    Department (February-May 1865)
Battles: Little Rock Campaign (August-September 1863)
Pine Bluff (October 25. 1863)
Red River Campaign (March-May 1864)
Further Reading: Bailey, Anne J., *Between the Enemy and Texas: Parson's
Texas Cavalry in the Civil War.*

179. TEXAS 22ND CAVALRY REGIMENT

Nickname: 1st Indian-Texas Cavalry Regiment
Organization: Organized in early 1862. Dismounted in 1862. Surrendered
by General E. K. Smith, commanding Trans-Mississippi Department, on May
26, 1865.
First Commander: Robert H. Taylor (Colonel)
Field Officers: John A. Buck (Major, Lieutenant Colonel)
William H. Johnson (Lieutenant Colonel)
Thomas Lewelling (Lieutenant Colonel)
George W. Merrick (Major, Lieutenant Colonel)
James G. Stevens (Major, Colonel)
Robert D. Stone (Major, Lieutenant Colonel)
Assignments: Department of the Indian Territory (May 1862)
Indian Territory, Trans-Mississippi Department (May-August 1862)
Cooper's Division, District of Arkansas, Trans-Mississippi Department (Au-
    gust-October 1862)
Bradfute's Brigade, Roane's Division, 1st Corps, Army of the West, Trans-Mis-
    sissippi Department (December 1862-January 1863)
Speight's Brigade, Steele's Division, District of Arkansas, Trans-Mississippi
    Department (January-April 1863)
Polignac's Brigade, District of West Louisiana, Trans-Mississippi Department
    (July-November 1863)
Polignac's Brigade, Mouton's-Polignac's Division, District of West Louisiana,
    Trans-Mississippi Department (November 1863-September 1864)
4th (King's) Texas Infantry Brigade, 2nd (Polignac's) Division, 1st Corps,
    Trans-Mississippi Department (September 1864-April 1865)
Bee's Brigade, Maxey's Division, District of Texas, New Mexico, and Arizona,
    Trans-Mississippi Department (April-May 1865)
Battles: Newtonia (September 30, 1862)

Red River Campaign (March-May 1864)
Harrisonburg (March 2, 1864)
Mansfield (April 8, 1864)
Pleasant Hill (April 9, 1864)

180. TEXAS 23RD CAVALRY REGIMENT

Organization: Organized in early 1862. Dismounted in February 1865. Surrendered by General E. K. Smith, commanding Trans-Mississippi Department, on May 26, 1865.
First Commander: Nicholas C. Gould (Colonel)
Field Officers: William R. Caton (Major)
John A. Corley (Major, Lieutenant Colonel)
Isaac A. Grant (Lieutenant Colonel)
Assignments: District of Texas, Trans-Mississippi Department (August-December 1862)
District of Texas, New Mexico, and Arizona, Trans-Mississippi Department (December 1862-January 1863)
Eastern Sub-district, District of Texas, New Mexico, and Arizona, Trans-Mississippi Department (January 1863-March 1864)
Hawes'-Major's-Debray's Brigade, Green's-Wharton's Cavalry Division, District of West Louisiana, Trans-Mississippi Department (March-September 1864)
6th (Debray's) Texas Cavalry Brigade, 2nd (Maxey's) Texas Cavalry Division, 1st Corps, Trans-Mississippi Department (September 1864-February 1865)
Robertson's Brigade, Maxey's Division, District of Texas, New Mexico, and Arizona, Trans-Mississippi Department (April-May 1865)
Battles: Red River Campaign (March-May 1864)
Mansfield (April 8, 1864)
Pleasant Hill (April 9, 1864)

181. TEXAS 24TH CAVALRY REGIMENT

Nickname: 2nd Texas Lancers
Organization: Organized from part of the 21st Texas Cavalry Regiment at Hempstead on April 24, 1862. Dismounted at Pine Bluff, Arkansas in June or July 1862. Surrendered at Arkansas Post on January 11, 1863. Exchanged in April 1863. Field consolidation with the 25th Cavalry Regiment from July 1863 to April 9, 1865. Additional field consolidation with the 17th and 18th Cavalry Regiments from July 1864 to April 9, 1865. Consolidated with the 6th, 7th, and 10th Infantry Regiments and the 15th, 17th, 18th, and 25th Cavalry Regiments (dismounted) and designated as the 1st Infantry Regiment Consolidated at Smithfield, North Carolina on April 9, 1865. Detachment surren-

dered by General E. K. Smith, commanding Trans-Mississippi Department, on May 26, 1865.

First Commander: Francis C. Wilkes (Colonel)

Field Officers: Robert Neyland (Lieutenant Colonel)

Patrick H. Swearingen (Major, Lieutenant Colonel)

William A. Taylor (Major, Colonel)

Assignments: Carter's Cavalry Brigade, Eastern District, Department of Texas (April-May 1862)

Carter's Cavalry Brigade, Eastern District of Texas, Trans-Mississippi Department (May-August 1862)

Carter's Cavalry Brigade, District of Arkansas, Trans-Mississippi Department (August-September 1862)

Garland's Brigade, 1st Corps, Army of the West, Trans-Mississippi Department (September-December 1862)

Garland's Brigade, Churchill's Division, District of Arkansas, Trans-Mississippi Department (December 1862-January 1863)

Churchill's-Deshler's-Smith's Brigade, Cleburne's Division, 2nd Corps, Army of Tennessee (May-November 1863)

Smith's-Granbury's Brigade, Cleburne's Division, 1st Corps, Army of Tennessee (November 1863-April 1865)

Headquarters, Trans-Mississippi Department [detachment] (September 1864-May 1865)

Battles: Arkansas Post (January 4-11, 1863)

Chickamauga (September 19-20, 1863)

Chattanooga Siege (September-November 1863)

Chattanooga (November 23-25, 1863)

Atlanta Campaign (May-September 1864)

Pickett's Mill (May 27, 1864)

New Hope Church (June 27, 1864)

Atlanta Siege (July-September 1864)

Jonesboro (August 31-September 1, 1864)

Franklin (November 30, 1864)

Nashville (December 15-16, 1864)

Carolinas Campaign (February-April 1865)

Bentonville (March 19-21, 1865)

Further Reading: Brown, Norman D., ed., *One of Cleburne's Command: The Civil War Reminiscences and Diary of Capt. Samuel T. Foster, Granbury's Texas Brigade, CSA.*

182. TEXAS 25TH CAVALRY REGIMENT

Nickname: 3rd Texas Lancers

Organization: Organized from part of the 21st Texas Cavalry Regiment at Hempstead on April 24, 1862. Dismounted at Pine Bluff, Arkansas in June or July 1862. Surrendered at Arkansas Post on January 11, 1863. Exchanged in April 1863. Field consolidation with the 24th Cavalry Regiment from July 1863 to April 9, 1865. Additional field consolidation with the 17th and 18th Cavalry Regiments from July 1864 to April 9, 1865. Consolidated with the 6th, 7th, and 10th Infantry Regiments and the 15th, 17th, 18th, and 24th Cavalry Regiments (dismounted) and designated as the 1st Infantry Regiment Consolidated at Smithfield, North Carolina on April 9, 1865. Detachment surrendered by General E. K. Smith, commanding Trans-Mississippi Department, on May 26, 1865.

First Commander: Clayton C. Gillespie (Colonel)

Field Officers: Joseph N. Dark (Major)

William N. Neyland (Lieutenant Colonel)

Edward B. Pickett (Major)

Assignments: Carter's Cavalry Brigade, Eastern District, Department of Texas (April-May 1862)

Carter's Cavalry Brigade, Eastern District of Texas, Trans-Mississippi Department (May-August 1862)

Carter's Cavalry Brigade, District of Arkansas, Trans-Mississippi Department (August-September 1862)

Garland's Brigade, 1st Corps, Army of the West, Trans-Mississippi Department (September-December 1862)

Garland's Brigade, Churchill's Division, District of Arkansas, Trans-Mississippi Department, Trans-Mississippi Department (December 1862-January 1863)

Churchill's-Deshler's-Smith's Brigade, Cleburne's Division, 2nd Corps, Army of Tennessee (May-November 1863)

Smith's-Granbury's Brigade, Cleburne's Division, 1st Corps, Army of Tennessee (November 1863-April 1865)

Headquarters, Trans-Mississippi Department [detachment] (September 1864-May 1865)

Battles: Arkansas Post (January 4-11, 1863)

Chickamauga (September 19-20, 1863)

Chattanooga Siege (September-November 1863)

Chattanooga (November 23-25, 1863)

Atlanta Campaign (May-September 1864)

Pickett's Mill (May 27, 1864)

New Hope Church (June 27, 1864)

Atlanta Siege (July-September 1864)

Jonesboro (August 31-September 1, 1864)

Franklin (November 30, 1864)

Nashville (December 15-16, 1864)
Carolinas Campaign (February-April 1865)
Bentonville (March 19-21, 1865)

183. TEXAS 26TH CAVALRY REGIMENT

Nickname: The Menagerie

Organization: Organized by the increase of the 7th Cavalry Battalion to a regiment on March 17, 1862. Surrendered by General E. K. Smith, commanding Trans-Mississippi Department, on May 26, 1865.

First Commander: Samuel B. Davis (Colonel)

Field Officers: Xavier B. Debray (Colonel)

Medard Menard (Major, Lieutenant Colonel)

John J. Myers (Lieutenant Colonel, Colonel)

George W. Owens (Major)

Assignments: Eastern District, Department of Texas (March-May 1862)

Sub-district of Houston, Eastern District of Texas, Trans-Mississippi Department (May-August 1862)

Sub-district of Houston, District of Texas, Trans-Mississippi Department (August-December 1862)

District of Texas, New Mexico, and Arizona, Trans-Mississippi Department (December 1862-January 1863)

Eastern Sub-district, District of Texas, New Mexico, and Arizona, Trans-Mississippi Department (January-November 1863)

Debray's Brigade, Eastern Sub-district, District of Texas, New Mexico, and Arizona, Trans-Mississippi Department (November-December 1863)

Debray's Cavalry Brigade, Slaughter's Division [or Eastern Sub-district], District of Texas, New Mexico, and Arizona, Trans-Mississippi Department (December 1863-March 1864)

Hawes'-Major's-Debray's Brigade, Green's-Wharton's Cavalry Division, District of West Louisiana, Trans-Mississippi Department (March-September 1864)

6th (Debray's) Texas Cavalry Brigade, 2nd (Maxey's) Texas Cavalry Division, 1st Corps, Trans-Mississippi Department (September 1864-February 1865)

Debray's Brigade, Bee's Division, Wharton's Cavalry Corps, Trans-Mississippi Department (February-May 1865)

Battles: Galveston Island (January 1, 1863)

Red River Campaign (March-May 1864)

Mansfield (April 8, 1864)

Pleasant Hill (April 9, 1864)

Further Reading: Debray, Xavier B., *A Sketch of the History of Debray's 26th Regiment of Texas Cavalry.*

184.   TEXAS 27TH CAVALRY REGIMENT

Nicknames: Whitfield's Legion,

Organization: Organized with 12 companies by the increase of the 4th Cavalry Battalion to a regiment in early 1862.   Dismounted in April 1862. Remounted in October 1862.   Surrendered by Lieutenant General Richard Taylor, commanding the Department of Alabama, Mississippi, and East Louisiana, at Citronelle, Alabama on May 4, 1865.

First Commander: John W. Whitfield (Colonel)

Field Officers: John H. Broocks (Major, Lieutenant Colonel)

Edwin R. Hawkins (Lieutenant Colonel, Colonel)

Cyrus K. Holman (Major)

B. H. Norsworthy (Major)

John T. Whitfield (Major)

Assignments: Hébert's Brigade, Price's Division, Trans-Mississippi District, Department #2 (April 1862)

Hébert's Brigade, Price's-Little's Division, Army of the West, Department #2 (April-July 1862)

Hébert's Brigade, Little's-Hébert's-Green's Division, Price's Corps, Army of West Tennessee, Department #2 (September-October 1862)

Griffith's-Whitfield's Cavalry Brigade, Maury's Division, Price's Corps, Army of West Tennessee, Department of Mississippi and East Louisiana (October-December 1862)

Whitfield's Brigade, 2nd Division, Van Dorn's Cavalry Corps, Department of Mississippi and East Louisiana (January-February 1863)

Whitfield's Brigade, Jackson's Division, Van Dorn's Cavalry Corps, Department of Mississippi and East Louisiana (February 1863)

Whitfield's Brigade, Jackson's Division, Van Dorn's Cavalry Corps, Army of Tennessee (February-May 1863)

Whitfield's Brigade, Jackson's Cavalry Division, Department of the West (June-July 1863)

Whitfield's Brigade, Jackson's Cavalry Division, Department of Mississippi and East Louisiana (July-August 1863)

Whitfield's-Ross' Brigade, Jackson's Division, Lee's Cavalry Corps, Department of Mississippi and East Louisiana (August 1863-January 1864)

Ross' Brigade, Jackson's Division, Lee's Cavalry Corps, Department of Alabama, Mississippi, and East Louisiana (January-May 1864)

Ross' Brigade, Jackson's Cavalry Division, Army of Mississippi (May-July 1864)

Ross' Brigade, Jackson's Cavalry Division, Army of Tennessee (July 1864-February 1865)

Ross' Brigade, Jackson's Division, Forrest's Cavalry Corps, Department of Alabama, Mississippi, and East Louisiana (February-May 1865)

Battles: Corinth Campaign (April-June 1862)
Iuka (September 19, 1862)
Corinth (October 3-4, 1862)
Oakland [skirmish] (December 3, 1862)
Holly Springs (December 20, 1862)
Davis' Mills (December 21, 1862)
Middleburg (December 24, 1862)
Yazoo Pass (February 16-19, 1863)
Thompson's Station (March 5, 1863)
Vicksburg Campaign (May-July 1863)
Jackson Siege (July 1863)
Meridian Campaign (February-March 1864)
Atlanta Campaign (May-September 1864)
Atlanta Siege (July-September 1864)
Flat Shoals (July 28, 1864)
Franklin-Nashville Campaign (October 1864-January 1865)

185.   TEXAS 28TH CAVALRY REGIMENT

Organization: Organized in the spring of 1862. Dismounted in 1862. Surrendered by General E. K. Smith, commanding Trans-Mississippi Department, on May 26, 1865.
First Commander: Horace Randal (Colonel)
Field Officers: Eli H. Baxter, Jr. (Lieutenant Colonel, Colonel)
Henry G. Hall (Major, Lieutenant Colonel)
Patrick Henry (Major)
Assignments: Eastern District of Texas, Department of Texas (May 1862)
Eastern District of Texas, Trans-Mississippi Department (May-August 1862)
Randal's Brigade, McCulloch's Division, District of Arkansas, Trans-Mississippi Department (September 1862)
Randal's Brigade, McCulloch's Division, 2nd Corps, Trans-Mississippi Department (September 1862-January 1863)
Randal's Brigade, McCulloch's-Walker's Division, District of Arkansas, Trans-Mississippi Department (February-March 1863)
Randal's Brigade, Walker's Division, District of West Louisiana, Trans-Mississippi Department (May 1863-April 1864)
Randal's-Maclay's Brigade, Walker's Division, District of Arkansas, Trans-Mississippi Department (April-May 1864)
Maclay's Brigade, Walker's Division, District of West Louisiana, Trans-Mississippi Department (May-September 1864)
3rd (Maclay's) Texas Brigade, 1st (Forney's) Texas Division, 1st Corps, Trans-Mississippi Department (September 1864-May 1865)

Battles: Milliken's Bend (June 7, 1863)
Harrisonburg (September 4, 1863)
Red River Campaign (March-May 1864)
Camden Expedition (March-May 1864)
Mansfield (April 8, 1864)
Pleasant Hill (April 9, 1864)
Jenkins' Ferry (April 30, 1864)

186. TEXAS 29TH CAVALRY REGIMENT

Organization: Organized in July 1862. Dismounted in February 1865. Surrendered by General E. K. Smith, commanding Trans-Mississippi Department, on May 26, 1865. Disbanded at Camp Grace, near Hempstead in May 1865.

First Commander: Charles De Morse (Colonel)

Field Officers: Joseph A. Carroll (Major)

Otis G. Welch (Lieutenant Colonel)

Assignments: Cooper's Brigade, Roane's Division, 1st Corps, Army of the West, Trans-Mississippi Department (December 1862-January 1863)

Cooper's Brigade, Steele's Cavalry Division, District of Arkansas, Trans-Mississippi Department (January-October 1863)

Cooper's Brigade, Indian Territory, Trans-Mississippi Department (October 1863-February 1864)

DeMorse's Brigade, Indian Territory, Trans-Mississippi Department (February 1864)

Gano's Brigade, Maxey's Cavalry Division, District of Arkansas, Trans-Mississippi Department (April 1864)

District of the Indian Territory, Trans-Mississippi District (July 1864)

Gano's Brigade, Cooper's (Indian) Division, District of the Indian Territory, Trans-Mississippi Department (September 1864)

Gano's Brigade, Cooper's (Indian) Division, Wharton's Cavalry Corps, Trans-Mississippi Department (September 1864-February 1865)

1st (Waul's) Texas Infantry Brigade, 1st (Forney's) Texas Infantry Division, 1st Corps, Trans-Mississippi Department (February-May 1865)

Battles: Fort Gibson (May 20, 1863)

near Honey Springs (July 17, 1863)

Camden Expedition (March-May 1864)

Poison Spring (April 18, 1864)

Camden (April 23, 1864)

Massard's Prairie, near Fort Smith [detachment] (July 27, 1864)

Cabin Creek (September 19, 1864)

Further Reading: Felmly, Bradford K. and Grady, John C., *Suffering To Silence: 29th Texas Cavalry, CSA Regimental History.*

187.   TEXAS 30TH CAVALRY REGIMENT

Also Known As: 1st Texas Partisan Rangers

Organization: Organized in mid-1862. Surrendered by General E. K. Smith, commanding Trans-Mississippi Department, on May 26, 1865.

First Commander: Edward J. Gurley (Colonel)

Field Officers: Nicholas W. Battle (Lieutenant Colonel)

John H. Davenport (Major)

Assignments: Eastern District of Texas, Trans-Mississippi Department (August 1862)

District of Texas, Trans-Mississippi Department (August-December 1862)

District of Texas, New Mexico, and Arizona, Trans-Mississippi Department (December 1862-January 1863)

Eastern Sub-district, District of Texas, New Mexico, and Arizona, Trans-Mississippi Department (January-June 1863)

Northern Sub-district, District of Texas, New Mexico, and Arizona, Trans-Mississippi Department (June-August 1863)

Cooper's Brigade, Department of the Indian Territory (November 1863)

Gano's Brigade, Maxey's Cavalry Division, District of Arkansas, Trans-Mississippi Department (February-July 1864)

District of the Indian Territory, Trans-Mississippi Department (July 1864)

5th (Gano's) Texas Cavalry Brigade, 2nd (Maxey's) Texas Cavalry Division, 1st Corps, Trans-Mississippi Department (September 1864-February 1865)

Parsons' Brigade, Steele's Division, Wharton's Cavalry Corps, Trans-Mississippi Department (February-May 1865)

Battles: Camden Expedition (March-May 1864)

Poison Spring (April 18, 1864)

Massard's Prairie, near Fort Smith [detachment] (July 27, 1864)

Fort Gibson (September 16, 1864)

Cabin Creek (September 19, 1864)

Further Reading: Bailey, Anne J., *Between the Enemy and Texas: Parson's Texas Cavalry in the Civil War.*

188.   TEXAS 31ST CAVALRY REGIMENT

Also Known As: Guess' Cavalry Battalion

Organization: Organized in April 1862. Dismounted in 1862. Surrendered by General E. K. Smith, commanding Trans-Mississippi Department, on May 26, 1865.

First Commander: Trezevant C. Hawpe (Colonel)

Field Officers: George W. Guess (Lieutenant Colonel)

Peter Hardeman (Colonel)

Frederick J. Malone (Major, Colonel)

William W. Peak (Major)

Edward Riordan (Lieutenant Colonel)

Assignments: Cooper's Division, District of Arkansas, Trans-Mississippi Department (September-October 1862)

Bradfute's Brigade, Roane's Division, 1st Corps, Trans-Mississippi Department (December 1862-January 1863)

Department of the Indian Territory, Trans-Mississippi Department (January-June 1863)

Speight's Brigade, District of Western Louisiana, Trans-Mississippi Department (June-September 1863)

Polignac's Brigade, District of West Louisiana, Trans-Mississippi Department (November 1863)

Polignac's-King's Brigade, Mouton's-Polignac's Division, District of West Louisiana, Trans-Mississippi Department (November 1863-September 1864)

4th (King's) Texas Brigade, 2nd (Polignac's) Division, 1st Corps, Trans-Mississippi Department (September 1864-February 1865)

Harrison's Brigade, District of Texas, New Mexico, and Arizona, Trans-Mississippi Department (March-April 1865)

Bee's Brigade, Maxey's Division, District of Texas, New Mexico, and Arizona, Trans-Mississippi Department (April-May 1865)

Battles: Newtonia (September 30, 1862)

Stirling's Plantation (September 29, 1863)

Red River Campaign (March-May 1864)

189.   TEXAS 31ST (HARDEMAN'S) CAVALRY REGIMENT

See: TEXAS 1ST CAVALRY REGIMENT, ARIZONA BRIGADE

190.   TEXAS 32ND CAVALRY REGIMENT

Also Known As: 15th Cavalry Regiment

Organization: Organized by the increase of the 1st Cavalry Battalion to a regiment in May 1862. Surrendered by Lieutenant General Richard Taylor, commanding the Department of Alabama, Mississippi, and East Louisiana, at Citronelle, Alabama on May 4, 1865. This regiment served dismounted throughout its career.

First Commander: Julius A. Andrews (Colonel)

Field Officers: William E. Estes (Major)

James A. Weaver (Lieutenant Colonel)

Assignments: Hogg's-Cabell's Brigade, McCown's Division, Army of the West, Department #2 (May-July 1862)

Ector's Brigade, McCown's Division, Department of East Tennessee (July-August 1862)

Ector's Brigade, McCown's Division, Army of Kentucky, Department #2 (August-October 1862)

Ector's Brigade, McCown's Division, Department of East Tennessee (October-November 1862)

Ector's Brigade, McCown's Division, 3rd (E. K. Smith's) Corps, Army of Tennessee (November 1862-March 1863)

Ector's Brigade, McCown's Division, 1st Corps, Army of Tennessee (March-May 1863)

Ector's Brigade, Walker's Division, Department of the West (June-July 1863)

Ector's Brigade, Walker's Division, Department of Mississippi and East Louisiana (July-August 1863)

Ector's Brigade, Walker's Division, Reserve Corps, Army of Tennessee (August-September 1863)

Ector's Brigade, French's Division, Department of Mississippi and East Louisiana (October 1863-January 1864)

Ector's Brigade, French's Division, Department of Alabama, Mississippi, and East Louisiana (January-May 1864)

Ector's Brigade, French's Division, Army of Mississippi (May-July 1864)

Ector's Brigade, French's Division, 3rd Corps, Army of Tennessee (July 1864-January 1865)

Ector's Brigade, French's Division, District of the Gulf, Department of Alabama, Mississippi, and East Louisiana (February-April 1865)

Ector's Brigade, French's Division, Department of Alabama, Mississippi, and East Louisiana (April 1865)

Battles: Corinth Campaign (April-June 1862)

Kentucky Campaign (August-October 1862)

Richmond (August 30, 1862)

Murfreesboro (December 31, 1862-January 3, 1863)

Vicksburg Campaign (May-July 1863)

Jackson (May 14, 1863)

Jackson Siege (July 1863)

Chickamauga (September 19-20, 1863)

Meridian Campaign (February-March 1864)

Atlanta Campaign (May-September 1864)

Cassville (May 19-22, 1864)

Kennesaw Mountain (June 27, 1864)

Peach Tree Creek (July 20, 1864)

Atlanta (July 22, 1864)

Atlanta Siege (July-September 1864)

Jonesboro (August 31-September 1, 1864)

Lovejoy's Station (September 2, 1864)

Allatoona (October 5, 1864)
Franklin (November 30, 1864)
Nashville (December 15-16, 1864)
Mobile (March 17-April 12, 1865)
Fort Blakely (April 1-9, 1865)

191. TEXAS 32ND (SWEET'S) CAVALRY REGIMENT
See: TEXAS 15TH CAVALRY REGIMENT

192. TEXAS 32ND (WOODS') CAVALRY REGIMENT
See: TEXAS 36TH CAVALRY REGIMENT

193. TEXAS 33RD CAVALRY REGIMENT
Organization: Organized by the increase of the 14th Cavalry Battalion to a
regiment in early 1863. Surrendered by General E. K. Smith, commanding
Trans-Mississippi Department, on May 26, 1865.
First Commander: James Duff (Colonel)
Field Officers: Santos Benavides (Major)
John T. Brackenridge (Major)
John L. Robinson (Major)
James R. Sweet (Lieutenant Colonel)
Assignments: Western Sub-district, District of Texas, New Mexico, and
   Arizona, Trans-Mississippi Department (May 1863-March 1864)
Northern Sub-district, District of Texas, New Mexico, and Arizona, Trans-Mis-
   sissippi Department (April-September 1864)
5th (Gano's) Texas Cavalry Brigade, 2nd (Maxey's) Texas Cavalry Brigade, 1st
   Corps, Trans-Mississippi Department (September 1864-February 1865)
Hardeman's Brigade, Bee's Division, Wharton's Cavalry Corps, Trans-Missis-
   sippi Department (February-May 1865)
Battles: Point Isabel (May 30, 1863)
near Mier *vs.* Zapata (September 2, 1863)
Harrisonburg (March 2, 1864)
Palmetto Ranch (May 12-13, 1865)

194. TEXAS 34TH (ALEXANDER'S) CAVALRY REGIMENT
Also Known As: 2nd Partisan Rangers Regiment
Organization: Organized at Fort Washita, Indian Territory on April 17, 1862.
Dismounted prior to September 30, 1864. Surrendered by General E. K. Smith,
commanding Trans-Mississippi Department, on May 26, 1865.
First Commander: Almerine M. Alexander (Colonel)
Field Officers: William M. Bush (Major, Lieutenant Colonel)

John H. Caudle (Lieutenant Colonel, Colonel)

M. W. Deavenport (Major)

Thomas Dove (Major)

John R. Russell (Major, Lieutenant Colonel)

Sevier Tackett (Major)

George H. Wooten (Lieutenant Colonel)

Assignments: Indian Territory, Trans-Mississippi District, Department #2 (April-May 1862)

Department of the Indian Territory, Trans-Mississippi Department (May-September 1862)

Cooper's Brigade, 1st Corps, Trans-Mississippi Department (September-December 1862)

Bradfute's Brigade, Roane's Division, 1st Corps, Trans-Mississippi Department (December 1862-January 1863)

Department of the Indian Territory, Trans-Mississippi Department (January-June 1863)

Speight's Brigade, District of Western Louisiana, Trans-Mississippi Department (June-September 1863)

Polignac's Brigade, District of Western Louisiana, Trans-Mississippi Department (November 1863)

Polignac's Brigade, Mouton's-Polignac's Division, District of Western Louisiana, Trans-Mississippi Department (November 1863-September 1864)

4th Texas Brigade, Polignac's Division, 1st Corps, Trans-Mississippi Department (September 1864-May 1865)

Battles: Prairie Grove (December 7, 1862)

Newtonia (September 30, 1862)

Stirling's Plantation (September 29, 1863)

Red River Campaign (March-May 1864)

Atchafalaya River (September 17, 1864)

Bayou Ala and Morgan's Ferry (September 20, 1864)

Further Reading: Weddle, Robert S., *Plow-Horse Cavalry: The Caney Creek Boys of the 34th Cavalry.*

195. TEXAS 34TH (TERRELL'S) CAVALRY REGIMENT

See: TEXAS TERRELL'S CAVALRY REGIMENT

196. TEXAS 34TH (WELLS') CAVALRY REGIMENT

See: TEXAS WELLS' CAVALRY REGIMENT

197. TEXAS 35TH (BROWN'S) CAVALRY REGIMENT

Organization: Organized by the consolidation of the 12th and Rountree's Cavalry Battalions in the summer of 1863. Surrendered by General E. K. Smith, commanding Trans-Mississippi Department, on May 26, 1865.

First Commander: Reuben R. Brown (Colonel)

Field Officers: Samuel W. Perkins (Lieutenant Colonel)

Lee C. Rountree (Major)

Assignments: Buchel's Brigade, Slaughter's Division [or Eastern Sub-district], District of Texas, New Mexico, and Arizona, Trans-Mississippi Department (September 1863-February 1864)

1st Sub-district, District of Texas, New Mexico, and Arizona, Trans-Mississippi Department (April-September 1864)

8th (McCulloch's) Texas Cavalry Brigade, 3rd (Draytons') Texas Cavalry Division, 3rd Corps, Trans-Mississippi Department (September 1864-February 1865)

Hardeman's Brigade, Bee's Division, Wharton's Cavalry Corps, Trans-Mississippi Department (February-May 1865)

198. TEXAS 35TH (LIKENS') CAVALRY REGIMENT

Organization: Organized by the consolidation of Likens' and Burns' Cavalry Battalions on October 23, 1863, per S.O. #168, Adjutant and Inspector General's Office. Reorganized in November 1863. Dismounted in March 1865. Surrendered by General E. K. Smith, commanding Trans-Mississippi Department, on May 26, 1865. Disbanded at Harrisburg ca. May 27, 1865.

First Commander: James B. Likens (Colonel)

Field Officers: James R. Burns (Lieutenant Colonel)

William A. Wortham (Major)

Assignments: Luckett's Brigade, District of Texas, New Mexico, and Arizona, Trans-Mississippi Department (November-December 1863)

Duff's Brigade, Bee's Division [or Western Sub-district, District of Texas, New Mexico, and Arizona, Trans-Mississippi Department (December 1863)

Western Sub-district, District of Texas, New Mexico, and Arizona, Trans-Mississippi Department (January-March 1864)

Bee's Brigade, Green's-Major's Cavalry Division, District of West Louisiana, Trans-Mississippi Department (March-September 1864)

4th (Bagby's) Texas Cavalry Brigade, 2nd (Maxey's) Texas Cavalry Division, 1st Corps, Trans-Mississippi Department (September 1864-March 1865)

Harrison's Brigade, Maxey's Division, District of Texas, New Mexico, and Arizona, Trans-Mississippi Department (March-April 1865)

Robertson's Brigade, Maxey's Division, District of Texas, New Mexico, and Arizona, Trans-Mississippi Department (April-May 1865)

Battles: Red River Campaign (March-May 1864)
Mansfield (April 8, 1864)
Pleasant Hill (April 9, 1864)
Atchafalaya River (September 17, 1864)
Bayou Ala and Morgan's Ferry (September 20, 1864)

199. TEXAS 36TH CAVALRY REGIMENT

Also Known As: 32nd Cavalry Regiment
Organization: Organized in the summer of 1862. Surrendered by General E. K. Smith, commanding Trans-Mississippi Department, on May 26, 1865.
First Commander: Peter C. Woods (Colonel)
Field Officers: Nathaniel Benton (Lieutenant Colonel)
Stokely M. Holmes (Major)
William O. Hutchinson (Major, Lieutenant Colonel)
Assignments: Sub-district of the Rio Grande, District of Texas, Trans-Mississippi Department (August-December 1862)
District of Texas, New Mexico, and Arizona, Trans-Mississippi Department (December 1862-January 1863)
Western Sub-district, District of Texas, New Mexico, and Arizona, Trans-Mississippi Department (January-March 1864)
Bee's Brigade, Major's-Green's Cavalry Division, District of West Louisiana, Trans-Mississippi Department (March-May 1864)
6th (Debray's) Texas Cavalry Brigade, 2nd (Maxey's) Texas Cavalry Division, 1st Corps, Trans-Mississippi Department (September 1864-March 1865)
Debray's Brigade, Bee's Division, Wharton's Cavalry Corps, Trans-Mississippi Department (March-May 1865)
Battles: Red River Campaign (March-May 1864)
Mansfield (April 8, 1864)
Pleasant Hill (April 9, 1864)

200. TEXAS 46TH CAVALRY REGIMENT

See: TEXAS FRONTIER CAVALRY REGIMENT

201. TEXAS ANDERSON'S-BORDER'S CAVALRY REGIMENT

Organization: Organized by the consolidation of the Cadet and Border's Cavalry Battalions in April 1864. Dismounted in March 1865. Surrendered by General E. K. Smith, commanding Trans-Mississippi Department, on May 26, 1865.
First Commander: Thomas S. Anderson (Colonel)
Field Officers: John P. Border (Lieutenant Colonel, Colonel)
Philip Fulcrod (Lieutenant Colonel)

Daniel Egbert (Major)

James A. Randle (Major)

Assignments: 3rd Sub-district, District of Texas, New Mexico, and Arizona, Trans-Mississippi Department (April-September 1864)

7th (Slaughter's) Texas Cavalry Brigade, 3rd (Drayton's) Texas Cavalry Division, 3rd Corps, Trans-Mississippi Department (September 1864-March 1865)

Bee's Brigade, Maxey's Division, District of Texas, New Mexico, and Arizona, Trans-Mississippi Department (March-May 1865)

202. TEXAS BENAVIDES' CAVALRY REGIMENT

Organization: Organized in the summer of 1864. Surrendered by General E. K. Smith, commanding Trans-Mississippi Department, on May 26, 1865.

First Commander: Santos Benavides (Colonel)

Field Officer: Mat Nolan (Lieutenant Colonel)

Assignments: Western Sub-district, District of Texas, New Mexico, and Arizona, Trans-Mississippi Department (August-September 1864)

7th (Slaughter's) Texas Cavalry Brigade, 3rd (Drayton's) Texas Cavalry Division, 3rd Corps, Trans-Mississippi Department (September 1864-May 1865)

Battles: Laredo (March 19, 1864)

Palmetto Ranch (May 12-13, 1865)

203. TEXAS BORDER CAVALRY BATTALION

Organization: Organized in the summer of 1863. Increased to a regiment and designated as the Border Cavalry Regiment in early 1864.

First Commander: James Bourland (Lieutenant Colonel)

Assignment: Northern Sub-district, District of Texas, New Mexico, and Arizona, Trans-Mississippi Department (August 1863-February 1864)

204. TEXAS BORDER CAVALRY REGIMENT

Organization: Organized by the increase of the Border Cavalry Battalion to a regiment in early 1864. Surrendered by General E. K. Smith, commanding Trans-Mississippi Department, on May 26, 1865.

First Commander: James Bourland (Colonel)

Field Officers: John R. Diamond (Lieutenant Colonel)

Charles L. Roff (Major)

Assignments: Northern Sub-district, District of Texas, New Mexico, and Arizona, Trans-Mississippi Department (March-September 1864)

8th (McCulloch's) Texas Cavalry Brigade, 3rd (Drayton's) Texas Cavalry Division, 3rd Corps, Trans-Mississippi Department (September 1864-May 1865)

Battle: Elm Creek (October 13, 1864)

205. TEXAS BORDER'S CAVALRY BATTALION

Organization: Organized in early 1864. Consolidated with the Cadet Cavalry Battalion and designated as Anderson's [later Border's] Cavalry Regiment in April 1864.
First Commander: John P. Border (Lieutenant Colonel)
Assignment: 3rd Sub-district, District of Texas, New Mexico, and Arizona, Trans-Mississippi Department (April 1864)

206. TEXAS BORDER'S CAVALRY REGIMENT

See: TEXAS ANDERSON'S-BORDER'S CAVALRY REGIMENT

207. TEXAS BRADFORD'S-MANN'S CAVALRY REGIMENT

Organization: Organized in the spring of 1864. Surrendered by General E. K. Smith, commanding Trans-Mississippi Department, on May 26, 1865.
First Commander: Charles M. Bradford (Colonel)
Field Officers: Thomas R. Hoxey (Major)
Walter L. Mann (Lieutenant Colonel, Colonel)
John E. Oliver (Major)
William F. Upton (Lieutenant Colonel)
Assignments: Western Sub-district, District of Texas, New Mexico, and Arizona, Trans-Mississippi Department (June-September 1864)
8th (McCulloch's) Texas Cavalry Brigade, 3rd (Drayton's) Texas Cavalry Division, 3rd Corps, Trans-Mississippi Department (September 1864-March 1865)
Defenses of Galveston, District of Texas, New Mexico, and Arizona, Trans-Mississippi Department (March-May 1865)

208. TEXAS BURNS' CAVALRY BATTALION

Organization: Organized in 1863. Consolidated with Likens' Cavalry Battalion and designated as the 35th (Likens') Cavalry Regiment on October 23, 1863, per S.O. #168, Adjutant and Inspector General's Office. This battalion does not appear in the *Official Records.*
First Commander: James R. Burns (Lieutenant Colonel)

209. TEXAS CADET CAVALRY BATTALION

Also Known As: Fulcrod's Cavalry Battalion
Organization: Organized in January 1864. Consolidated with Border's Cavalry Battalion and designated as Anderson's [later Border's] Cavalry Regiment in April 1864.

First Commander: Philip Fulcrod (Lieutenant Colonel)
Assignment: 3rd Sub-district, District of Texas, New Mexico, and Arizona, Trans-Mississippi Department (January-April 1864)

210. TEXAS CATER'S CAVALRY BATTALION

Organization: Organized in mid-1864. Apparently disbanded after August 1864.
First Commander: Thomas C. Cater (Major)
Assignment: Western Sub-district, District of Texas, New Mexico, and Arizona, Trans-Mississippi Department (August 1864)

211. TEXAS DALY'S-RAGSDALE'S CAVALRY BATTALION

Organization: Organized with five companies ca. January 1864. Dismounted in February 1865. Surrendered by General E. K. Smith, commanding Trans-Mississippi Department, on May 26, 1865.
First Commander: Andrew Dale (Lieutenant Colonel)
Field Officer: Samuel G. Ragsdale (Major, Lieutenant Colonel)
Assignments: Eastern Sub-district, District of Texas, New Mexico, and Arizona, Trans-Mississippi Department (January-September 1864)
Unattached, 3rd (Drayton's) Texas Cavalry Division, 3rd Corps, Trans-Mississippi Department (September 1864-February 1865)
6th (Hébert's) Texas Infantry Brigade, 2nd (Hébert's) Texas Infantry Division, 3rd Corps, Trans-Mississippi Department (February-May 1865)
Battle: Calcasieu Pass (May 6, 1864)

212. TEXAS FRONTIER CAVALRY REGIMENT

Also Known As: 46th Cavalry Regiment
Organization: Organized with nine companies in state service for 12 months on March 15, 1862 under an act for the defense of the Indian frontier of the state dated December 21, 1861. Mustered into Confederate service in 1864. Surrendered by General E. K. Smith, commanding Trans-Mississippi Department, on May 26, 1865.
First Commander: James N. Norris (Colonel)
Field Officers: W. J. Alexander (Major)
James B. Barry (Lieutenant Colonel)
James E. McCord (Major, Colonel)
Alfred T. Obershein (Lieutenant Colonel)
Assignments: Western District of Texas, Trans-Mississippi Department (March-August 1862)
District of Texas, Trans-Mississippi Department (August-December 1862)

District of Texas, New Mexico, and Arizona, Trans-Mississippi Department (December 1862-January 1863)

Western Sub-district, District of Texas, New Mexico, and Arizona, Trans-Mississippi Department (January-June 1863)

Northern Sub-district, District of Texas, New Mexico, and Arizona, Trans-Mississippi Department (June 1863-September 1864)

8th (McCulloch's) Texas Cavalry Brigade, 3rd (Drayton's) Texas Cavalry Division, 3rd Corps, Trans-Mississippi Department (September 1864-May 1865)

Battle: Dove Creek (January 8, 1865)

213. TEXAS FULCROD'S CAVALRY BATTALION
See: TEXAS CADET CAVALRY BATTALION

214. TEXAS GANO'S CAVALRY SQUADRON
Organization: Organized with two companies in mid-1862. Assigned to the 7th Kentucky Cavalry Regiment on September 1, 1862.
First Commander: Richard M. Gano (Captain)
Assignment: Morgan's Cavalry Brigade, Department of East Tennessee (July-September 1862)
Battles: Morgan's 1st Kentucky Raid (July 4-28, 1862)
Gallatin (August 12-13, 1862)
Morgan's Raid on the Louisville & Nashville Railroad (August 1862)
Kentucky Campaign (August-October 1862)

215. TEXAS GIDDINGS' CAVALRY BATTALION
Organization: Organized with six companies in the spring of 1864. Surrendered by General E. K. Smith, commanding Trans-Mississippi Department, on May 26, 1865.
First Commander: George H. Giddings (Lieutenant Colonel)
Assignment: Western Sub-district, District of Texas, New Mexico, and Arizona, Trans-Mississippi Department (June 1864-May 1865)
Battles: Rancho Las Rinas [skirmish] (June 25, 1864)
Palmetto Ranch (May 12-13, 1865)

216. TEXAS GILLETT'S CAVALRY BATTALION
Organization: Organized in mid-1863. Consolidated with Good's and Wells' Cavalry Battalions and designated as Wells' Cavalry Regiment in early 1865.
First Commander: L. E. Gillett (Major)
Assignment: Cooper's Brigade, Steele's Division, District of Arkansas, Trans-Mississippi Department (July 1863)

217. TEXAS GOOD'S CAVALRY BATTALION

Organization: Organized in the summer of 1864. Consolidated with Gillett's and Wells' Cavalry Battalions and designated as Wells' Cavalry Regiment in early 1865.
First Commander: Chaplin Good (Lieutenant Colonel)
Assignments: Northern Sub-district, District of Texas, New Mexico, and Arizona, Trans-Mississippi Department (August-September 1864)
5th (Gano's) Texas Cavalry Brigade, 2nd (Maxey's) Texas Cavalry Division, 1st Corps, Trans-Mississippi Department (September 1864-January 1865)

218. TEXAS GUESS' CAVALRY BATTALION

See: TEXAS 30TH CAVALRY REGIMENT

219. TEXAS HARDEMAN'S CAVALRY BATTALION, ARIZONA BRIGADE

Organization: Organized with six companies in early 1863. Increased to a regiment and designated as the 1st Cavalry Regiment, Arizona Brigade on February 21, 1863. This battalion does not appear in the *Official Records.*
First Commander: Peter Hardeman (Lieutenant Colonel)

220. TEXAS HEAD'S CAVALRY BATTALION

Organization: Organized in early 1864. Apparently disbanded later in 1864.
First Commander: J. W. Head (Major)
Assignment: De Morse's Brigade, Maxey's Division, District of the Indian Territory, Trans-Mississippi Department (April 1864)

221. TEXAS HERBERT'S CAVALRY BATTALION, ARIZONA BRIGADE

Nickname: Arizona Battalion
Organization: Organized with three companies in late 1862. Broken up in May 1863. NOTE: This unit is filed at the National Archives as an Arizona unit; the only one.
First Commander: Philemon T. Herbert (Lieutenant Colonel)
Field Officer: George M. Frazer (Major)

222. TEXAS LIKENS' CAVALRY BATTALION

Organization: Organized in 1863. Consolidated with Burns' Cavalry Battalion and designated as the 35th (Likens') Cavalry Regiment on October 23, 1863 per S.O. #168, Adjutant and Inspector General's Office. This battalion does not appear separately in the *Official Records.*

First Commander: James B. Likens (Major, Lieutenant Colonel)

223. TEXAS MCKIE'S CAVALRY SQUADRON
See: TEXAS MORGAN'S CAVALRY BATTALION [OF WHICH IT WAS A PART]

224. TEXAS MANN'S CAVALRY REGIMENT
See: TEXAS BRADFORD'S-MANN'S CAVALRY REGIMENT

225. TEXAS MORGAN'S CAVALRY BATTALION
Organization: Organized with three companies in the spring of 1862. Increased to nine companies. Increased to a regiment but not recognized by the War Department and designated as Morgan's Cavalry Regiment in March 1865.
First Commander: Charles L. Morgan (Major, Lieutenant Colonel)
Field Officer: B. C. McKie (Major)
Assignments: Unattached, Trans-Mississippi District,Trans-Mississippi Department (May-August 1862)
Unattached, District of Arkansas, Trans-Mississippi Department (August-September 1862)
Carter's Brigade, Marmaduke's Cavalry Division, District of Arkansas, Trans-Mississippi Department (April-July 1863)
Carter's Brigade, Walker's Cavalry Division, District of Arkansas, Trans-Mississippi Department (July-October 1863)
Carter's-Parsons' Cavalry Brigade, District of Arkansas, Trans-Mississippi Department (October 1863-March 1864)
Carter's-Parson's Brigade, Steele's Cavalry Division, District of West Louisiana, Trans-Mississippi Department (March-September 1864)
1st (Steele's) Texas Cavalry Brigade, 1st (Wharton's) Cavalry Division, 2nd Corps, Trans-Mississippi Department (September 1864-February 1865)
Parsons' Brigade, Steele's Division, Wharton's Cavalry Corps, Trans-Mississippi Department (February-March 1865)
Battles: Marmaduke's Expedition into Missouri (April 27-May 2, 1863)
Little Rock Campaign (August-September 1863)
Pine Bluff (October 25. 1863)
Further Reading: Bailey, Anne J., *Between the Enemy and Texas: Parson's Texas Cavalry in the Civil War.*

226. TEXAS MORGAN'S CAVALRY REGIMENT
Organization: Organized by the increase of Morgan's Cavalry Battalion to a regiment in March 1865. However this conversion was not recognized by the

War Department. Surrendered by General E. K. Smith, commanding Trans-Mississippi Department, on May 26, 1865.

First Commander: Charles L. Morgan (Colonel)

Field Officers: Milton W. Boggess (Major)

Samuel J. Richardson (Lieutenant Colonel)

Assignment: Parsons' Brigade, Steele's Division, Wharton's Cavalry Corps, Trans-Mississippi Department (March-May 1865)

227. TEXAS MULLEN'S CAVALRY BATTALION, ARIZONA BRIGADE

Organization: Organized in early 1863. Two companies consolidated with the 2nd Cavalry Battalion, Arizona Brigade and two independent companies and designated as the 2nd Cavalry Regiment, Arizona Brigade on February 21, 1863. This battalion does not appear in the *Official Records.*

First Commander: John W. Mullen (Lieutenant Colonel)

228. TEXAS RAGSDALE'S CAVALRY BATTALION

See: TEXAS DALY'S-RAGSDALE'S CAVALRY BATTALION

229. TEXAS ROUNTREE'S CAVALRY BATTALION

Organization: Organized by the assignment of two companies from the 13th Infantry Regiment in the summer of 1862. Increased to four companies. Consolidated with the 12th Cavalry Battalion and designated as the 35th (Brown's) Cavalry Regiment in the fall of 1863.

First Commander: Lee C. Rountree (Major)

Assignments: Western Sub-district of Texas, Trans-Mississippi Department (August 1862)

District of Texas, Trans-Mississippi Department (August-December 1862)

District of Texas, New Mexico, and Arizona, Trans-Mississippi Department (December 1862-May 1863)

Unattached, Sub-district of Southwestern Louisiana, District of West Louisiana, Trans-Mississippi Department (September 1863)

Battle: Stirling's Plantation (September 29, 1863)

230. TEXAS SAUFLEY'S SCOUTING CAVALRY BATTALION

Organization: This battalion does not appear in the *Official Records.*

First Commander: William P. Saufley (Major)

231. TEXAS SCANLAND'S CAVALRY SQUADRON

See: TEXAS WELLS' CAVALRY BATTALION

232. TEXAS SOUTH KANSAS-TEXAS CAVALRY REGIMENT
See: TEXAS 3RD CAVALRY REGIMENT

233. TEXAS TERRELL'S CAVALRY BATTALION
Organization: Organized in 1863. Increased to a regiment and designated as Terrell's Cavalry Regiment in 1864.
First Commander: Alexander W. Terrell (Lieutenant Colonel)
Further Reading: Spencer, John W., *Terrell's Texas Cavalry*.

234. TEXAS TERRELL'S CAVALRY REGIMENT
Also Known As: 34th Cavalry Regiment
37th Cavalry Regiment
Organization: Organized by the increase of Terrell's Cavalry Battalion to a regiment in 1863. Reorganized in November 1863. Surrendered by General E. K. Smith, commanding Trans-Mississippi Department, on May 26, 1865. Disbanded at Wild Cat Bluff in May 1865.
First Commander: Alexander W. Terrell (Colonel)
Field Officers: Hiram S. Morgan (Major)
George W. Owens (Major)
John C. Robertson (Lieutenant Colonel)
Assignments: Northern Sub-district, District of Texas, New Mexico, and Arizona, Trans-Mississippi Department (July 1863)
Eastern Sub-district, District of Texas, New Mexico, and Arizona, Trans-Mississippi Department (September-November 1863)
Buchel's Brigade, Eastern Sub-district, District of Texas, New Mexico, and Arizona, Trans-Mississippi Department (November-December 1863)
Debray's Brigade, Slaughter's Division [or Eastern Sub-district], District of Texas, New Mexico, and Arizona, Trans-Mississippi Department (December 1863-January 1864)
Eastern Sub-district, District of Texas, New Mexico, and Arizona, Trans-Mississippi Department (January-March 1864)
Bee's Brigade, Green's Cavalry Division, District of West Louisiana, Trans-Mississippi Department (March-September 1864)
4th (Bagby's) Texas Cavalry Brigade, 2nd (Maxey's) Texas Cavalry Division, 1st Corps, Trans-Mississippi Department (September 1864-February 1865)
Battles: Red River Campaign (March-May 1864)
Mansfield (April 8, 1864)
Pleasant Hill (April 9, 1864)
Atchafalaya River (September 17, 1864)
Bayou Ala and Morgan's Ferry (September 20, 1864)
Further Reading: Spencer, John W., *Terrell's Texas Cavalry*.

235. TEXAS TERRY'S CAVALRY REGIMENT

Organization: Organized in early 1864. Dismounted in February 1865. Surrendered by General E. K. Smith, commanding Trans-Mississippi Department, on May 26, 1865.

First Commander: David S. Terry (Colonel)

Field Officers: S. H. Brooks (Lieutenant Colonel)

J. M. Evans (Major)

Assignments: Western Sub-district, District of Texas, New Mexico, and Arizona, Trans-Mississippi Department (April-May 1864)

Eastern Sub-district, District of Texas, New Mexico, and Arizona, Trans-Mississippi Department (May-September 1864)

Northern Sub-district, District of Texas, New Mexico, and Arizona, Trans-Mississippi Department [one company] (August-September 1864)

Bee's Brigade, Maxey's Division, District of Texas, New Mexico, and Arizona, Trans-Mississippi Department (April-May 1865)

236. TEXAS TERRY'S TEXAS RANGERS CAVALRY REGIMENT

See: TEXAS 8TH CAVALRY REGIMENT

237. TEXAS WAUL'S LEGION CAVALRY BATTALION

Organization: Organized with six companies at Brenham in early 1862. Detached from the Legion in early 1863. Detachment surrendered at Vicksburg, Warren County, Mississippi on July 4, 1863. Detachment paroled at Vicksburg, Warren County, Mississippi in July 1863. Detachment declared exchanged on September 12, 1863. Surrendered by Lieutenant General Richard Taylor, commanding the Department of Alabama, Mississippi, and East Louisiana, at Citronelle, Alabama on May 4, 1865.

First Commander: Leonidas M. Willis (Major, Lieutenant Colonel)

Field Officers: Thomas M. Harwood (Major)

H. S. Parker (Major)

John R. Smith (Major)

Benjamin F. Weeks (Major)

Assignments: Eastern District of Texas, Trans-Mississippi Department (May-August 1862)

Waul's Legion, Lovell's Division, District of the Mississippi, Department #2 (September-October 1862)

Waul's Legion, Loring's Division, Lovell's Corps, Army of West Tennessee, Department of Mississippi and East Louisiana (October-December 1862)

Waul's Legion, Loring's Division, Lovell's Corps, Army of North Mississippi, Department of Mississippi and East Louisiana (December 1862-January 1863)

Waul's Legion, Loring's Division, Army of the Department of Mississippi and East Louisiana (January 1863)

Waul's Legion, 2nd Military District, Department of Mississippi and East Louisiana (January-March 1863)

Moore's Brigade, Loring's Division, 2nd Military District, Department of Mississippi and East Louisiana (April 1863)

Moore's Brigade, Loring's Division, Department of Mississippi and East Louisiana [detachment] (April 1863)

Waul's Legion, Stevenson's Division, Department of Mississippi and East Louisiana [detachment] (April-July 1863)

McCulloch's Cavalry Brigade, 5th Military District, Department of Mississippi and East Louisiana (May-September 1863)

Chalmers' Cavalry Brigade, Department of Mississippi and East Louisiana (September-October 1863)

McCulloch's Brigade, Chalmers' Cavalry Division, Department of Mississippi and East Louisiana (October-November 1863)

McCulloch's Brigade, Chalmers' Division, Lee's Cavalry Corps, Department of Mississippi and East Louisiana (November 1863-January 1864)

McCulloch's Brigade, Chalmers' Division, Lee's Cavalry Corps, Department of Mississippi and East Louisiana (January 1864)

McCulloch's Brigade, Chalmers' Division, Forrest's Cavalry Corps, Department of Mississippi and East Louisiana (January 1864)

McCulloch's-Wade's-McCulloch's Brigade, Chalmers' Division, Forrest's Cavalry Corps, Department of Alabama, Mississippi, and East Louisiana (January-September 1864)

McCulloch's Cavalry Brigade, District of the Gulf, Department of Alabama, Mississippi, and East Louisiana (September-October 1864)

McCulloch's Cavalry Brigade, Liddell's Division, District of the Gulf, Department of Alabama, Mississippi, and East Louisiana (October-November 1864)

McCulloch's Cavalry Brigade, District of the Gulf, Department of Alabama, Mississippi, and East Louisiana (November 1864-February 1865)

Ross' Brigade, Jackson's Division, Forrest's Cavalry Corps, Department of Alabama, Mississippi, and East Louisiana (February-May 1865)

Battles: Vicksburg Campaign (May-July 1863)

Vicksburg Siege [detachment] (May-July 1863)

Tupelo (July 14, 1864)

Smith's 2nd Mississippi Invasion (August 1864)

Abbeville [skirmish] (August 23, 1864)

Chickasawha Bridge (December 10, 1864)

Wilson's Raid (March-April 1865)

238. TEXAS WELLS' CAVALRY BATTALION

Organization: Organized in the summer of 1863. Consolidated with Good's and Gillett's Cavalry Battalions and designated as Wells' Cavalry Regiment in early 1865.

First Commander: John W. Wells (Lieutenant Colonel)

Assignments: Cooper's Brigade, District of the Indian Territory, Trans-Mississippi Department (August-October 1863)

District of the Indian Territory, Trans-Mississippi Department (October 1863-September 1864)

5th (Gano's) Texas Cavalry Brigade, 2nd (Maxey's) Texas Cavalry Division, 1st Corps, Trans-Mississippi Department (September 1864-January 1865)

Battles: Hahn's Farm, near Waldron [skirmish] (June 19, 1864)

Massard's Prairie, near Fort Smith (July 27, 1864)

239. TEXAS WELLS' CAVALRY REGIMENT

Also Known As: 34th Cavalry Regiment

Organization: Organized by the consolidation of Gillett's, Good's, and Wells' Cavalry Battalions in early 1865. Surrendered by General E. K. Smith, commanding Trans-Mississippi Department, on May 26, 1865.

First Commander: John W. Wells (Colonel)

Field Officers: L. E. Gillett (Major)

Chaplin Good (Lieutenant Colonel)

Assignment: Northern Sub-district, District of Texas, New Mexico, and Arizona, Trans-Mississippi Department (May 1865)

240. TEXAS WHITFIELD'S CAVALRY LEGION

See: TEXAS 27TH CAVALRY REGIMENT

INFANTRY

241.   TEXAS 1ST INFANTRY BATTALION

Organization: Organized in McLennan County in 1861. Increased to a regiment and designated as the 15th Infantry Regiment ca. August 1862.
First Commander: James W. Speight (Lieutenant Colonel)
Field Officer: James E. Harrison (Major)
Assignments: Department of Texas (December 1861-May 1862)
Trans-Mississippi Department (May-August 1862)

242.   TEXAS 1ST INFANTRY BATTALION, SHARPSHOOTERS

Organization: Organized with five companies in Grayson County in 1862. When serving west of the Mississippi this battalion served mounted at times. Surrendered by General E. K. Smith, commanding Trans-Mississippi Department, on May 26, 1865.
First Commander: James Burnet (Major)
Assignments: Maxey's Brigade, 3rd Military District, Department of Mississippi and East Louisiana (March-May 1863)
Maxey's Brigade, Loring's Division, Department of the West (May-June 1863)
Maxey's Brigade, French's Division, Department of the West (June-July 1863)
Maxey's Brigade, French's Division, Department of Mississippi and East Louisiana (July-September 1863)
Quarles' Brigade, Department of the Gulf (September-November 1863)
Unattached, Indian Territory, District of Arkansas, Trans-Mississippi Department (February-July 1864)
Unattached, District of the Indian Territory, Trans-Mississippi Department (July-September 1864)
Unattached, Cooper's Indian Cavalry Division, Trans-Mississippi Department (September 1864-May 1865)
Battles: Capture of the *Indianola* (February 24, 1863)
Vicksburg Campaign (May-July 1863)

Jackson Siege (July 1863)

243. TEXAS 1ST INFANTRY BATTALION, STATE TROOPS

Organization: Organized for six months in late 1863. Mustered out in early 1864.

First Commander: Marcus G. Settle (Lieutenant Colonel)

Field Officer: J. B. Anderson (Major)

Assignment: Northern Sub-District, District of Texas, New Mexico, and Arizona, Trans-Mississippi Department (October 1863-January 1864)

244. TEXAS 1ST INFANTRY REGIMENT

Organization: Organized with 12 companies, part for 12 months and part for the war in August 1861. Reorganized for the war on May 19, 1862. Surrendered at Appomattox Court House, Virginia on April 9, 1865.

First Commander: Louis T. Wigfall (Colonel)

Field Officers: Frederick S. Bass (Major, Lieutenant Colonel, Colonel)

Harvey H. Black (Major, Lieutenant Colonel)

Albert G. Clopton (Major, Lieutenant Colonel)

Matt Dale (Major)

Richard J. Harding (Major, Lieutenant Colonel)

Hugh McLeod (Major, Lieutenant Colonel, Colonel)

Alexis T. Rainey (Major, Lieutenant Colonel, Colonel)

John R. Woodward (Major)

Phillip A. Work (Lieutenant Colonel)

Assignments: Texas Brigade, Forces Near Dumfries [Whiting's Command], 2nd Corps, Potomac District, Department of Northern Virginia (October 1861-February 1862)

Texas Brigade, Forces Near Dumfries [Whiting's Command], Potomac District, Department of Northern Virginia (February-March 1862)

Texas Brigade, Whiting's-G. W. Smith's-Whiting's Division, Army of Northern Virginia (March-June 1862)

Texas Brigade, Whiting's Division, Valley District, Department of Northern Virginia (June 1862)

Texas Brigade, Whiting's Division, 2nd Corps, Army of Northern Virginia (June-July 1862)

Texas Brigade, Whiting's-Hood's Division, 1st Corps, Army of Northern Virginia (July 1862-February 1863)

Texas Brigade, Hood's Division, Department of North Carolina and Southern Virginia (February-April 1863)

Texas Brigade, Hood's Division, Department of Southern Virginia (April-May 1863)

Texas Brigade, Hood's Division, 1st Corps, Army of Northern Virginia (May-September 1863)

Texas Brigade, Hood's Division, Longstreet's Corps, Army of Tennessee (September-November 1863)

Texas Brigade, Hood's-Field's Division, Department of East Tennessee (November 1863-April 1864)

Texas Brigade, Field's Division, 1st Corps, Army of Northern Virginia (April 1864-April 1865)

Battles: Freestone Point (September 25, 1861)

Occoquan [skirmish] (February 28, 1862)

Eltham Landing (May 7, 1862)

Seven Pines (May 31-June 1, 1862)

Seven Days Battles (June 25-July 1, 1862)

Gaines' Mill (June 27, 1862)

Malvern Hill (July 1, 1862)

Freeman's Ford (August 21, 1862)

Thoroughfare Gap (August 28, 1862)

2nd Bull Run (August 28-30, 1862)

South Mountain (September 14, 1862)

Antietam (September 17, 1862)

Fredericksburg (December 13, 1862)

Washington Siege (March-April 1863)

Washington (April 4, 1863)

Suffolk Campaign (April 1863)

Gettysburg (July 1-3, 1863)

Front Royal [skirmish] (July 22, 1863)

Chickamauga (September 19-20, 1863)

Chattanooga Siege (September-November 1863)

Wauhatchie (October 28-29, 1863)

Knoxville Siege (November-December 1863)

The Wilderness (May 5-6, 1864)

Spotsylvania Court House (May 8-21, 1864)

North Anna (May 23-26, 1864)

Cold Harbor (June 1-3, 1864)

Petersburg Siege (June 1864-April 1865)

New Market Heights (September 29, 1864)

Chaffin's Farm (September 29, 1864)

Fort Gilmer (September 29-30, 1864)

Williamsburg Road (October 27, 1864)

Appomattox Court House (April 9, 1865)

Further Reading: Simpson, Harold B., *Hood's Texas Brigade: Lee's Grenadier Guard.* Simpson, Harold B., *The History of Hood's Texas Brigade, 1861- 1865.*

245. TEXAS 1ST INFANTRY REGIMENT, CONSOLIDATED

Organization: Organized by the consolidation of the 6th, 7th, and 10th Infantry Regiments and the 15th, 17th, 18th, 24th, and 25th Cavalry Regiments [dismounted] at Smithfield, North Carolina on April 9, 1865.
Field Officer: William A. Ryan (Lieutenant Colonel)
Assignment: Govan's Brigade, Brown's Division, 1st Corps, Army of Tennessee (April 1865)
Battle: Carolinas Campaign (February-April 1865)

246. TEXAS 1ST INFANTRY REGIMENT, STATE TROOPS

Organization: Organized for six months in late 1863. Mustered out in early 1864.
First Commander: Kerr B. DeWalt (Colonel)
Field Officers: L. G. Cleveland (Major)
Thomas B. Stubbs (Lieutenant Colonel)
Assignment: A. Smith's Brigade, Eastern Sub-district, District of Texas, New Mexico, and Arizona, Trans-Mississippi Department (December 1863-January 1864)

247. TEXAS 2ND INFANTRY BATTALION

Organization: This battalion does not appear in the *Official Records.*
First Commander: Leonidas M. Martin (Colonel)

248. TEXAS 2ND INFANTRY REGIMENT

Also Known As: 2nd Sharpshooters
Organization: Organized at Galveston in late 1861. Regiment surrendered at Vicksburg, Warren County, Mississippi on July 4, 1863. Paroled at Vicksburg, Warren County, Mississippi in July 1863. Declared exchanged on September 12, 1863. Reorganized in Texas in the fall of 1863. Surrendered by General E. K. Smith, commanding Trans-Mississippi Department, on May 26, 1865.
First Commander: John C. Moore (Colonel)
Field Officers: Xavier B. Debray (Major)
George W. L. Fly (Major)
Noble L. McGinnis (Major, Lieutenant Colonel, Colonel)
William P. Rogers (Lieutenant Colonel, Colonel)
Hal G. Runnels (Major)
Ashbel Smith (Lieutenant Colonel, Colonel)
William C. Timmons (Major, Lieutenant Colonel)

J. F. Ward (Lieutenant Colonel)

Assignments: Department of Texas (December 1861-February 1862)

Jackson's Brigade, Withers' Division, 2nd Corps, Army of the Mississippi, Department #2 (March-May 1862)

Fagan's-Moore's Brigade, Ruggles' Division, 2nd Corps, Army of the Mississippi, Department #2 (May-June 1862)

Moore's Brigade, Maury's Division, Army of the West, Trans-Mississippi Department (June-August 1862)

Moore's Brigade, Maury's Division, Price's Corps, Army of West Tennessee, Department #2 (September-October 1862)

Moore's Brigade, Maury's Division, Price's Corps, Army of West Tennessee, Department of Mississippi and East Louisiana (October-December 1862)

Moore's Brigade, Maury's Division, Price's Corps, Army of North Mississippi, Department of Mississippi and East Louisiana (December 1862)

Moore's Brigade, Maury's-Forney's Division, 2nd Military District, Department of Mississippi and East Louisiana (December 1862-April 1863)

Moore's Brigade, Forney's Division, Department of Mississippi and East Louisiana (April-July 1863)

Luckett's-Waul's Brigade, Eastern Sub-district, District of Texas, New Mexico, and Arizona, Trans-Mississippi Department (November-December 1863)

Waul's Brigade, Slaughter's Division [or Eastern Sub-district], District of Texas, New Mexico, and Arizona, Trans-Mississippi Department (December 1863-January 1864)

Eastern Sub-district, District of Texas, New Mexico, and Arizona, Trans-Mississippi Department (January-February 1864)

Waul's Brigade, Walker's Division, District of West Louisiana, Trans-Mississippi Department (March-April 1864)

Waul's Brigade, Walker's Division, District of Arkansas, Trans-Mississippi Department (April 1864)

1st Sub-district (Hawes'), District of Texas, New Mexico, and Arizona, Trans-Mississippi Department (March-September 1864)

5th (Hawes') Texas Brigade, 2nd (Hébert's) Texas Division, 3rd Corps, Trans-Mississippi Department (September 1864-May 1865)

Battles: Shiloh (April 6-7, 1862)

Corinth Campaign (April-June 1862)

Farmington (May 9, 1862)

Iuka (September 19, 1862)

Corinth (October 3-4, 1862)

Hatchie Bridge (October 5, 1862)

Chickasaw Bayou (December 27-29, 1862)

Fort Pemberton (March 11-April 5, 1863)

Vicksburg Campaign (May-July 1863)
Champion's Hill (May 16, 1863)
Big Black River Bridge (May 17, 1863)
Vicksburg Siege (May-July 1863)
Red River Campaign (March-May 1864)
Mansfield (April 8, 1864)
Pleasant Hill (April 9, 1864)
Further Reading: Chance, Joseph E., *The Second Texas Infantry: From Shiloh to Vicksburg.*

249.   TEXAS 2ND INFANTRY REGIMENT, SHARPSHOOTERS
See: TEXAS 2ND INFANTRY REGIMENT

250.   TEXAS 2ND INFANTRY REGIMENT, STATE TROOPS
Organization: Organized for six months in late 1863. Mustered out in early 1864.
First Commander: Thompson Camp (Colonel)
Field Officers: William H. Parks (Major)
Franklin B. Sublett (Lieutenant Colonel)
Assignment: A. Smith's Brigade, District of Texas, New Mexico, and Arizona, Trans-Mississippi Department (December 1863-January 1864)

251.   TEXAS 3RD INFANTRY BATTALION
Organization: Organized for six months in late 1861. Mustered out in early 1862.
First Commander: J. E. Kirby (Major)
Assignments: Nichols Brigade, Department of Texas (February 1862)
Nichols Brigade, Eastern District of Texas, Department of Texas (February 1862)

252.   TEXAS 3RD INFANTRY REGIMENT
Organization: Organized in the summer of 1861. Surrendered by General E. K. Smith, commanding Trans-Mississippi Department, on May 26, 1865.
First Commander: Philip N. Luckett (Colonel)
Field Officers: Augustus Buchel (Lieutenant Colonel)
Edward F. Gray (Major, Lieutenant Colonel)
John F. Kampmann (Major)
Assignments: Department of Texas (September 1861-February 1862)
Eastern District of Texas, Department of Texas (February-May 1862)
Eastern District of Texas, Trans-Mississippi Department (May-August 1862)
District of Texas, Trans-Mississippi Department (August-December 1862)

District of Texas, New Mexico, and Arizona, Trans-Mississippi Department (December 1862-January 1863)

Eastern Sub-district, District of Texas, New Mexico, and Arizona, Trans-Mississippi Department (January-March 1863)

Luckett's Brigade, Scurry's Division [or Eastern Sub-district], District of Texas, New Mexico, and Arizona, Trans-Mississippi Department (June 1863)

Eastern Sub-district, District of Texas, New Mexico, and Arizona, Trans-Mississippi Department (June-November 1863)

Luckett's Brigade, Eastern Sub-district, District of Texas, New Mexico, and Arizona, Trans-Mississippi Department (November-December 1863)

Luckett's Brigade, Slaughter's Division [or Eastern Sub-district], District of Texas, New Mexico, and Arizona, Trans-Mississippi Department (December 1863-March 1864)

Scurry's Brigade, Walker's Division, District of West Louisiana, Trans-Mississippi Department (March-April 1864)

Scurry's Brigade, Walker's Division, District of Arkansas, Trans-Mississippi Department (April-May 1864)

Scurry's-Waterhouse's Brigade, Walker's Division, District of West Louisiana, Trans-Mississippi Department (May-September 1864)

2nd (Waterhouse's) Texas Brigade, 1st (Forney's) Texas Division, 1st Corps, Trans-Mississippi Department (September 1864-May 1865)

Battles: Red River Campaign (March-May 1864)

Camden Expedition (March-May 1864)

Mansfield (April 8, 1864)

Pleasant Hill (April 9, 1864)

Jenkins' Ferry (April 30, 1864)

253. TEXAS 3RD INFANTRY REGIMENT, STATE TROOPS

Organization: Organized for six months in late 1863. Mustered out in early 1864.

First Commander: Jesse T. Veal (Colonel)

Field Officer: J. B. Wilmeth (Colonel)

Assignment: A. Smith's Brigade, District of Texas, New Mexico, and Arizona, Trans-Mississippi Department (December 1863-January 1864)

254. TEXAS 4TH INFANTRY BATTALION

Nicknames: German Battalion,

Organization: Organized for six months in late 1861. Mustered out in early 1862.

First Commander: Theodore Oswald (Major)

Assignments: Nichols Brigade, Department of Texas (February 1862)

Nichols Brigade, Eastern District of Texas, Department of Texas (February 1862)

255. TEXAS 4TH INFANTRY REGIMENT

Organization: Organized by the War Department on September 30, 1861. Surrendered at Appomattox Court House, Virginia on April 9, 1865.

First Commander: John Bell Hood (Colonel)

Field Officers: John P. Bane (Major, Lieutenant Colonel, Colonel)
Benjamin F. Carter (Major, Lieutenant Colonel)
John C. G. Key (Major, Lieutenant Colonel, Colonel)
John Marshall (Major, Lieutenant Colonel)
William H. Martin (Major)
William P. Townsend (Major)
Clinton M. Walker (Major, Lieutenant Colonel)
Bradfute Warwick (Major, Lieutenant Colonel, Colonel)

Assignments: Texas Brigade, Forces Near Dumfries [Whiting's Command], 2nd Corps, Potomac District, Department of Northern Virginia (October 1861-February 1862)

Texas Brigade, Forces Near Dumfries [Whiting's Command], Potomac District, Department of Northern Virginia (February-March 1862)

Texas Brigade, Whiting's-G. W. Smith's-Whiting's Division, Army of Northern Virginia (March-June 1862)

Texas Brigade, Whiting's Division, Valley District, Department of Northern Virginia (June 1862)

Texas Brigade, Whiting's Division, 2nd Corps, Army of Northern Virginia (June-July 1862)

Texas Brigade, Whiting's-Hood's Division, 1st Corps, Army of Northern Virginia (July 1862-February 1863)

Texas Brigade, Hood's Division, Department of North Carolina and Southern Virginia (February-April 1863)

Texas Brigade, Hood's Division, Department of Southern Virginia (April-May 1863)

Texas Brigade, Hood's Division, 1st Corps, Army of Northern Virginia (May-September 1863)

Texas Brigade, Hood's Division, Longstreet's Corps, Army of Tennessee (September-November 1863)

Texas Brigade, Hood's-Field's Division, Department of East Tennessee (November 1863-April 1864)

Texas Brigade, Field's Division, 1st Corps, Army of Northern Virginia (April 1864-April 1865)

Battles: Eltham Landing (May 7, 1862)

Seven Pines (May 31-June 1, 1862)
Seven Days Battles (June 25-July 1, 1862)
Gaines' Mill (June 27, 1862)
Malvern Hill (July 1, 1862)
Freeman's Ford (August 21, 1862)
2nd Bull Run (August 28-30, 1862)
South Mountain (September 14, 1862)
Antietam (September 17, 1862)
Fredericksburg (December 13, 1862)
Washington Siege (March-April 1863)
Washington (April 4, 1863)
Suffolk Campaign (April 1863)
Gettysburg (July 1-3, 1863)
Chickamauga (September 19-20, 1863)
Chattanooga Siege (September-November 1863)
Wauhatchie (October 28-29, 1863)
Knoxville Siege (November-December 1863)
The Wilderness (May 5-6, 1864)
Spotsylvania Court House (May 8-21, 1864)
North Anna (May 23-26, 1864)
Cold Harbor (June 1-3, 1864)
Petersburg Siege (June 1864-April 1865)
New Market Heights (September 29, 1864)
Chaffin's Farm (September 29, 1864)
Fort Gilmer (September 29-30, 1864)
Williamsburg Road (October 27, 1864)
Appomattox Court House (April 9, 1865)
Further Reading: Simpson, Harold B., *Hood's Texas Brigade: Lee's Grenadier Guard.* Simpson, Harold B., *The History of Hood's Texas Brigade, 1861- 1865.*

256.   TEXAS 4TH INFANTRY REGIMENT, STATE TROOPS

Organization: Organized for six months in late 1863. Mustered out in early 1864.

First Commander: John Sayles (Colonel)

Field Officers: James W. Barnes (Lieutenant Colonel)

Moses A. Bryan (Major)

Assignment: A. Smith's Brigade, District of Texas, New Mexico, and Arizona, Trans-Mississippi Department (December 1863-January 1864)

257. TEXAS 5TH INFANTRY BATTALION

Organization: Organized in 1862. Increased to a regiment and designated as the 22nd Infantry Regiment in 1862.
First Commander: Richard B. Hubbard (Lieutenant Colonel)
Field Officer: Elias E. Lott (Major)

258. TEXAS 5TH INFANTRY REGIMENT

Organization: Organized by the War Department on October 1, 1861. Surrendered at Appomattox Court House, Virginia on April 9, 1865.
First Commander: James J. Archer (Colonel)
Field Officers: Walter B. Botts (Major, Lieutenant Colonel)
King Bryan (Major, Lieutenant Colonel)
Robert M. Powell (Major, Lieutenant Colonel, Colonel)
Paul J. Quattlebaum (Major)
Jerome B. Robertson (Lieutenant Colonel, Colonel)
Jefferson C. Rogers (Major)
John C. Upton (Major, Lieutenant Colonel)
David M. Whaley (Major)
Assignments: Texas Brigade, Forces Near Dumfries [Whiting's Command], 2nd Corps, Potomac District, Department of Northern Virginia (October 1861-February 1862)
Texas Brigade, Forces Near Dumfries [Whiting's Command], Potomac District, Department of Northern Virginia (February-March 1862)
Texas Brigade, Whiting's-G. W. Smith's-Whiting's Division, Army of Northern Virginia (March-June 1862)
Texas Brigade, Whiting's Division, Valley District, Department of Northern Virginia (June 1862)
Texas Brigade, Whiting's Division, 2nd Corps, Army of Northern Virginia (June-July 1862)
Texas Brigade, Whiting's-Hood's Division, 1st Corps, Army of Northern Virginia (July 1862-February 1863)
Texas Brigade, Hood's Division, Department of North Carolina and Southern Virginia (February-April 1863)
Texas Brigade, Hood's Division, Department of Southern Virginia (April-May 1863)
Texas Brigade, Hood's Division, 1st Corps, Army of Northern Virginia (May-September 1863)
Texas Brigade, Hood's Division, Longstreet's Corps, Army of Tennessee (September-November 1863)
Texas Brigade, Hood's-Field's Division, Department of East Tennessee (November 1863-April 1864)

Texas Brigade, Field's Division, 1st Corps, Army of Northern Virginia (April 1864-April 1865)

Battles: Eltham Landing (May 7, 1862)
Seven Pines (May 31-June 1, 1862)
Seven Days Battles (June 25-July 1, 1862)
Gaines' Mill (June 27, 1862)
Malvern Hill (July 1, 1862)
Freeman's Ford (August 21, 1862)
2nd Bull Run (August 28-30, 1862)
South Mountain (September 14, 1862)
Antietam (September 17, 1862)
Fredericksburg (December 13, 1862)
Washington Siege (March-April 1863)
Washington (April 4, 1863)
Suffolk Campaign (April 1863)
Gettysburg (July 1-3, 1863)
Chickamauga (September 19-20, 1863)
Chattanooga Siege (September-November 1863)
Wauhatchie (October 28-29, 1863)
Knoxville Siege (November-December 1863)
The Wilderness (May 5-6, 1864)
Spotsylvania Court House (May 8-21, 1864)
North Anna (May 23-26, 1864)
Cold Harbor (June 1-3, 1864)
Petersburg Siege (June 1864-April 1865)
New Market Heights (September 29, 1864)
Chaffin's Farm (September 29, 1864)
Fort Gilmer (September 29-30, 1864)
Williamsburg Road (October 27, 1864)
Appomattox Court House (April 9, 1865)
Further Reading: Simpson, Harold B., *Hood's Texas Brigade: Lee's Grenadier Guard.* Simpson, Harold B., *The History of Hood's Texas Brigade, 1861- 1865.*

259. TEXAS 5TH INFANTRY REGIMENT, STATE TROOPS

Organization: Organized for six months in late 1863. Mustered out in early 1864.
First Commander: Stephen H. Darden (Colonel)
Field Officers: William G. Jett (Lieutenant Colonel)
Albert Waltersdorff (Major)

Assignment: Duff's Brigade, Bee's Division, Western Sub-district [Bee], District of Texas, New Mexico, and Arizona, Trans-Mississippi Department (December 1863-February 1864)

260.   TEXAS 5TH (NICHOLS') INFANTRY REGIMENT
See: TEXAS 9TH (NICHOLS') INFANTRY REGIMENT

261.   TEXAS 6TH INFANTRY BATTALION
Organization: Organized in late 1861. Reorganized and designated as the 11th Cavalry and Infantry Battalion in April 1862.
First Commander: James B. Likens (Major)
Assignments: Department of Texas (December 1861-February 1862)
Eastern District, Department of Texas (February-April 1862)

262.   TEXAS 6TH INFANTRY REGIMENT
Organization: Organized in November 1861. Mustered into Confederate service at Camp Henry E. McCulloch, near Victoria, Victoria County in November 1861. Surrendered at Arkansas Post on January 11, 1863. Paroled and declared exchanged in April 1863. Field consolidation with the 10th Infantry Regiment and 15th Cavalry Regiment [dismounted] from July 1863 to April 9, 1865. The 10th Infantry Regiment was detached from this field consolidation between January and April 1864. Consolidated with the 7th and 10th Infantry Regiments and the 15th, 17th, 18th, 24th, and 25th Cavalry Regiments [dismounted] and designated as the 1st Infantry Regiment Consolidated at Smithfield, North Carolina on April 9, 1865.
First Commander: Robert R. Garland (Colonel)
Field Officers: Thomas S. Anderson (Lieutenant Colonel)
Rhoads Fisher (Major)
Alexander M. Haskell (Major)
Alexander H. Phillips, Jr. (Major)
Assignments: Department of Texas (October 1861-February 1862)
Western District, Department of Texas (February-May 1862)
Maury's Brigade, Jones' Division, Army of the West, Department #2 (May-July 1862)
District of Arkansas, Trans-Mississippi Department (August-September 1862)
Garland's Brigade, 1st Corps, Trans-Mississippi Department (September-December 1862)
Garland's Brigade, Churchill's Division, 2nd Corps, Trans-Mississippi Department (December 1862-January 1863)
Churchill's-Deshler's-Smith's-Granbury's Brigade, Cleburne's Division, 2nd Corps, Army of Tennessee (July-November 1863)

Granbury's Brigade, Cleburne's Division, 1st Corps, Army of Tennessee (November 1863-April 1865)

Battles: Corinth Campaign (April-June 1862)

Arkansas Post (January 4-11, 1863)

Chickamauga (September 19-20, 1863)

Chattanooga Siege (September-November 1863)

Chattanooga (November 23-25, 1863)

Atlanta Campaign (May-September 1864)

Pickett's Mill (May 27, 1864)

New Hope Church (June 27, 1864)

Atlanta Siege (July-September 1864)

Jonesboro (August 31-September 1, 1864)

Franklin (November 30, 1864)

Nashville (December 15-16, 1864)

Carolinas Campaign (February-April 1865)

Bentonville (March 19-21, 1865)

263. TEXAS 7TH INFANTRY BATTALION

See: TEXAS 7TH CAVALRY BATTALION

264. TEXAS 7TH INFANTRY REGIMENT

Organization: Organized in the summer of 1861. Surrendered at Fort Donelson on February 16, 1862. Exchanged ca. October 1862. Field consolidation with the 49th and 55th Tennessee Infantry Regiments and known as Bailey's Consolidated Regiment from October 1862 to early 1863. Consolidated with the 6th and 10th Infantry Regiments and the 15th, 17th, 18th, 24th, and 25th Cavalry Regiments [dismounted] and designated as the 1st Infantry Regiment. Consolidated at Smithfield, North Carolina on April 9, 1865.

First Commander: John Gregg (Colonel)

Field Officers: Jeremiah M. Clough (Lieutenant Colonel)

Hiram B. Granbury (Major, Lieutenant Colonel, Colonel)

William L. Moody (Major, Lieutenant Colonel, Colonel)

Khleber M. Van Zandt (Major)

Assignments: Department of Texas (September-October 1861)

Tilghman's-Clark's Brigade, Central Army of Kentucky, Department #2 (December 1861-February 1862)

Davidson's Brigade, Johnson's Division, Fort Donelson, Department #2 (February 1862)

Maxey's Brigade, Maury's Division, Price's Corps, Army of West Tennessee, Department of Mississippi and East Louisiana (October 1862)

Maxey's Brigade, District of East Louisiana, Department of Mississippi and East Louisiana (November 1862-February 1863)

Gregg's Brigade, District of East Louisiana, Department of Mississippi and East Louisiana (March-May 1863)

Gregg's Brigade, Department of the West (May-June 1863)

Gregg's Brigade, Walker's Division, Department of the West (June-July 1863)

Gregg's Brigade, Walker's Division, Department of Mississippi and East Louisiana (July-August 1863)

Gregg's Brigade, Johnson's Provisional Division, Army of Tennessee (September 1863)

Gregg's Brigade, Walker's Division, Longstreet's Corps, Army of Tennessee (September-November 1863)

Smith's-Granbury's Brigade, Cleburne's Division, 2nd Corps, Army of Tennessee (November 1863)

Granbury's Brigade, Cleburne's Division, 1st Corps, Army of Tennessee (November 1863-April 1865)

Battles: Fort Donelson (February 12-16, 1862)

vs. Grierson's Raid (April 17-May 2, 1863)

Vicksburg Campaign (May-July 1863)

Raymond (May 12, 1863)

Jackson (May 14, 1863)

Jackson Siege (July 1863)

Chickamauga (September 19-20, 1863)

Chattanooga Siege (September-November 1863)

Chattanooga (November 23-25, 1863)

Taylor's Ridge (November 27, 1863)

Atlanta Campaign (May-September 1864)

Pickett's Mill (May 27, 1864)

New Hope Church (June 27, 1864)

Atlanta Siege (July-September 1864)

Jonesboro (August 31-September 1, 1864)

Franklin (November 30, 1864)

Nashville (December 15-16, 1864)

Carolinas Campaign (February-April 1865)

Bentonville (March 19-21, 1865)

265. TEXAS 8TH INFANTRY BATTALION

Organization: Organized with four companies on May 14, 1862. Consolidated with the 4th Artillery Battalion and designated as the 8th Infantry Regiment in February 1863.

First Commander: Alfred M. Hobby (Major)

Assignments: Western District of Texas, Department of Texas (May 1862)
Western District of Texas, Trans-Mississippi Department (May-August 1862)
District of Texas, Trans-Mississippi Department (August-December 1862)
District of Texas, New Mexico, and Arizona, Trans-Mississippi Department
    (December 1862-January 1863)
Western Sub-district, District of Texas, New Mexico, and Arizona, Trans-Mississippi Department (January-February 1863)
Battle: Corpus Christie (August 16-18, 1862)

266. TEXAS 8TH INFANTRY REGIMENT

Organization: Organized by the consolidation of the 8th Infantry Battalion and the 4th Artillery Battalion in February 1863. Surrendered by General E. K. Smith, commanding Trans-Mississippi Department, on May 26, 1865.
First Commander: Alfred M. Hobby (Colonel)
Field Officers: John Ireland (Major, Lieutenant Colonel)
Daniel D. Shea (Lieutenant Colonel)
John A. Vernon (Major)
Assignments: Western Sub-district, District of Texas, New Mexico, and Arizona, Trans-Mississippi Department (February-June 1863)
1st Brigade, Bee's Division [or Western Sub-district], District of Texas, New Mexico, and Arizona, Trans-Mississippi Department (June 1863-October 1862)
Waul's Brigade, Slaughter's Division [or Eastern Sub-district], District of Texas, New Mexico, and Arizona, Trans-Mississippi Department (December 1863-March 1864)
Eastern [or 1st] Sub-district, District of Texas, New Mexico, and Arizona, Trans-Mississippi Department (April-September 1864)
6th (Hébert's) Texas Brigade, 2nd (Hébert's) Texas Division 3rd Corps, Trans-Mississippi Department (September 1864-April 1865)
Robertson's Brigade, Maxey's Division, District of Texas, New Mexico, and Arizona, Trans-Mississippi Department (April-May 1865)
Battles: Corpus Christie (August 16-18, 1862)
Saint Joseph's Island (May 3, 1863)

267. TEXAS 8TH (MAXEY'S) INFANTRY REGIMENT
See: TEXAS 9TH INFANTRY REGIMENT

268. TEXAS 8TH (YOUNG'S) INFANTRY REGIMENT
See: TEXAS 12TH INFANTRY REGIMENT

269. TEXAS 9TH (MAXEY'S) INFANTRY REGIMENT

Also Known As: 8th Infantry Regiment

Organization: Organized in late 1861. Surrendered by Lieutenant General Richard Taylor, commanding the Department of Alabama, Mississippi, and East Louisiana, at Citronelle, Alabama on May 4, 1865.

First Commander: Samuel B. Maxey (Colonel)

Field Officers: William E. Beeson (Lieutenant Colonel)

James Burnet (Major)

Miles A. Dillard (Lieutenant Colonel)

William M. Harrison (Major)

James H. McReynolds (Major)

Wright A. Stanley (Major, Colonel)

William H. Young (Colonel)

Assignments: Department of Texas (December 1861)

Department #2 (January 1862)

Pond's Brigade, 1st (Ruggles') Corps, 2nd Grand Division, Army of the Mississippi, Department #2 (March 1862)

Anderson's Brigade, Ruggles' Division, 2nd Corps, Army of the Mississippi, Department #2 (March-April 1862)

Maxey's Detached Brigade, 1st Corps, Army of the Mississippi, Department #2 (April-July 1862)

Maxey's Brigade, Cheatham's Division, Army of the Mississippi, Department #2 (July-August 1862)

Smith's Brigade, Cheatham's Division, Right Wing, Army of the Mississippi, Department #2 (August 1862)

Smith's Brigade, Cleburne's Division, Army of Kentucky, Department #2 (August-October 1862)

Smith's Brigade, Cheatham's Division, Right Wing, Army of the Mississippi, Department #2 (October-November 1862)

Smith's-Vaughan's Brigade, Cheatham's Division, 1st Corps, Army of Tennessee (November 1862-January 1863)

Ector's Brigade, McCown's Division, Department of East Tennessee (February-March 1863)

Ector's Brigade, McCown's Division, 1st Corps, Army of Tennessee (March-May 1863)

Ector's Brigade, Walker's Division, Department of the West (June-July 1863)

Ector's Brigade, Walker's Division, Department of Mississippi and East Louisiana (July-August 1863)

Ector's Brigade, Walker's Division, Reserve Corps, Army of Tennessee (August-September 1863)

Ector's Brigade, French's Division, Department of Mississippi and East Louisiana (October 1863-January 1864)

Ector's Brigade, French's Division, Department of Alabama, Mississippi, and East Louisiana (January-May 1864)

Ector's Brigade, French's Division, Army of Mississippi (May-July 1864)

Ector's Brigade, French's Division, 3rd Corps, Army of Tennessee (July 1864-January 1865)

Ector's Brigade, French's Division, District of the Gulf, Department of Alabama, Mississippi, and East Louisiana (February-April 1865)

Ector's Brigade, French's Division, Department of Alabama, Mississippi, and East Louisiana (April 1865)

Battles: Shiloh (April 6-7, 1862)

Corinth Campaign (April-June 1862)

Kentucky Campaign (August-October 1862)

Richmond (August 30, 1862)

Perryville (October 8, 1862)

Murfreesboro (December 31, 1862-January 3, 1863)

Vicksburg Campaign (May-July 1863)

Jackson (May 14, 1863)

Jackson Siege (July 1863)

Chickamauga (September 19-20, 1863)

Meridian Campaign (February-March 1864)

Atlanta Campaign (May-September 1864)

Cassville (May 19-22, 1864)

Kennesaw Mountain (June 27, 1864)

Peach Tree Creek (July 20, 1864)

Atlanta (July 22, 1864)

Atlanta Siege (July-September 1864)

Jonesboro (August 31-September 1, 1864)

Lovejoy's Station (September 2, 1864)

Allatoona (October 5, 1864)

Franklin (November 30, 1864)

Nashville (December 15-16, 1864)

Mobile (March 17-April 12, 1865)

Fort Blakely (April 1-9, 1865)

270. TEXAS 9TH (NICHOLS') INFANTRY REGIMENT

Also Known As: 5th Infantry Regiment

Organization: Organized for six months in late 1861. Mustered out of Confederate service in early 1862.

First Commander: Ebenezer B. Nichols (Colonel)

Field Officers: Josiah C. Massie (Lieutenant Colonel)
Frederick Tate (Major)
Assignments: Department of Texas (February 1862)
Nichols' Brigade, Eastern District of Texas, Department of Texas (February-March 1862)

271. TEXAS 10TH INFANTRY REGIMENT

Organization: Organized in the fall of 1861. Surrendered at Arkansas Post on January 11, 1863. Exchanged in April 1863. Field consolidation with the 6th Infantry Regiment and 15th Cavalry Regiment [dismounted] from July 1863 to January 1864. Consolidated with the 6th and 7th Infantry Regiments and the 15th, 17th, 18th, 24th, and 25th Cavalry Regiments [dismounted] and designated as the 1st Infantry Regiment. Consolidated at Smithfield, North Carolina on April 9, 1865.
First Commander: Allison Nelson (Colonel)
Field Officers: Seymour C. Brasher (Major)
John R. Kennard (Major)
Roger Q. Mills (Major, Lieutenant Colonel)
Robert B. Young (Lieutenant Colonel, Colonel)
Assignments: Department of Texas (October 1861-February 1862)
Nichols' Brigade, Eastern District, Department of Texas (February-March 1862)
Trans-Mississippi Department (May-August 1862)
District of Arkansas, Trans-Mississippi Department (August-September 1862)
Nelson's Brigade, Nelson's Division, 1st Corps, Trans-Mississippi Department (September-December 1862)
Deshler's Brigade, Churchill's Division, 2nd Corps, Trans-Mississippi Department (December 1862-January 1863)
Churchill's-Deshler's-Smith's-Granbury's Brigade, Cleburne's Division, 2nd Corps, Army of Tennessee (July-November 1863)
Granbury's Brigade, Cleburne's Division, 1st Corps, Army of Tennessee (November 1863-April 1865)
Battles: Arkansas Post (January 4-11, 1863)
Chickamauga (September 19-20, 1863)
Chattanooga Siege (September-November 1863)
Chattanooga (November 23-25, 1863)
Atlanta Campaign (May-September 1864)
Pickett's Mill (May 27, 1864)
New Hope Church (June 27, 1864)
Atlanta (July 22, 1864)
Atlanta Siege (July-September 1864)

Jonesboro (August 31-September 1, 1864)
Franklin (November 30, 1864)
Nashville (December 15-16, 1864)
Carolinas Campaign (February-April 1865)
Bentonville (March 19-21, 1865)

272.   TEXAS 11TH INFANTRY AND CAVALRY BATTALION

See: TEXAS 11TH CAVALRY AND INFANTRY BATTALION

273.   TEXAS 11TH INFANTRY REGIMENT

Organization: Organized in early 1862. Surrendered by General E. K. Smith, commanding Trans-Mississippi Department, on May 26, 1865.

First Commander: Oran M. Roberts (Colonel)

Field Officers: Nathaniel J. Caraway (Major)

A. J. Coupland (Lieutenant Colonel)

James H. Jones (Lieutenant Colonel, Colonel)

Thomas H. Rountree (Major)

Assignments: Eastern District of Texas, Department of Texas (May 1862)

Eastern District of Texas, Trans-Mississippi Department (May-August 1862)

Randal's Brigade, McCulloch's Division, District of Arkansas, Trans-Mississippi Department (September 1862)

Randal's Brigade, McCulloch's Division, 2nd Corps, Trans-Mississippi Department (September 1862-January 1863)

Randal's Brigade, McCulloch's-Walker's Division, District of Arkansas, Trans-Mississippi Department (February-March 1863)

Randal's Brigade, Walker's Division, District of West Louisiana, Trans-Mississippi Department (May 1863-April 1864)

Randal's-Maclay's Brigade, Walker's Division, District of Arkansas, Trans-Mississippi Department (April-May 1864)

Maclay's Brigade, Walker's Division, District of West Louisiana, Trans-Mississippi Department (May-September 1864)

3rd (Maclay's) Texas Brigade, 1st (Forney's) Texas Division, 1st Corps, Trans-Mississippi Department (September 1864-May 1865)

Battles: Bayou Bourbeau (November 3, 1863)

Red River Campaign (March-May 1864)

Camden Expedition (March-May 1864)

Mansfield (April 8, 1864)

Pleasant Hill (April 9, 1864)

Jenkins' Ferry (April 30, 1864)

274. TEXAS 12TH INFANTRY REGIMENT

Also Known As: 8th Infantry Regiment

Organization: Organized in early 1862. Surrendered by General E. K. Smith, commanding Trans-Mississippi Department, on May 26, 1865.

First Commander: Overton Young (Colonel)

Field Officers: William Clark (Major, Lieutenant Colonel)

Benjamin A. Philpott (Lieutenant Colonel)

James W. Raine (Major, Lieutenant Colonel)

Erastus W. Smith (Major)

Assignments: Eastern District of Texas, Department of Texas (February-May 1862)

Eastern District of Texas, Trans-Mississippi Department (May-August 1862)

Young's Brigade, McCulloch's Division, 2nd Corps, Trans-Mississippi Department (September 1862-January 1863)

Young's-Hawes' Brigade, McCulloch's-Walker's Division, District of Arkansas, Trans-Mississippi Department (February-March 1863)

Hawes'-Waul's Brigade, Walker's Division, District of West Louisiana, Trans-Mississippi Department (May 1863-April 1864)

Waul's Brigade, Walker's Division, District of Arkansas, Trans-Mississippi Department (April-May 1864)

Waul's Brigade, Walker's Division, District of Arkansas, Trans-Mississippi Department (May-September 1864)

1st (Waul's) Texas Brigade, 1st (Forney's) Texas Division, 1st Corps, Trans-Mississippi Department (September 1864-May 1865)

Battles: Young's Point (June 9, 1863)

Red River Campaign (March-May 1864)

Camden Expedition (March-May 1864)

Mansfield (April 8, 1864)

Pleasant Hill (April 9, 1864)

Jenkins' Ferry (April 30, 1864)

275. TEXAS 13TH INFANTRY REGIMENT

Also Known As: 4th Infantry Regiment

Nickname: Victoria Regiment

Organization: Organized with six companies of infantry and two each of artillery and cavalry in September and October 1861. Company D converted to artillery service and designated as Moseley's Artillery Battery on October 19, 1861. Two companies transferred to Rountree's Cavalry Battalion during the summer of 1862. Some companies transferred to the 12th Cavalry Battalion ca. July 1862. Balance of the regiment was designated as Bates' Infantry Battalion ca. July 1862. Reorganized as a regiment in early 1863. Company H became an independent artillery battery [which was later designated as the 16th Field Battery] on February 11, 1863. Company B was organized on June 14, 1863, but it was actually the Austin Grays Artillery Battery. Surrendered by General E. K. Smith, commanding Trans-Mississippi Department, on May 26, 1865.

First Commander: Joseph Bates (Colonel)

Field Officers: Reuben R. Brown (Lieutenant Colonel)

Henry P. Cayce (Lieutenant Colonel)

Robert L. Foard (Major)

Stephen S. Perry (Major)

Lee C. Rountree (Major)

Assignments: Department of Texas (October 1861-February 1862)

Western District of Texas, Department of Texas (February-May 1862)

Western District of Texas, Trans-Mississippi Department (May-July 1862)

Eastern Sub-district, District of Texas, New Mexico, and Arizona, Trans-Mississippi Department (February-December 1863)

Luckett's Brigade, Slaughter's Division [or Eastern Sub-district], District of Texas, New Mexico, and Arizona, Trans-Mississippi Department (December 1863-January 1864)

Eastern Sub-district, District of Texas, New Mexico, and Arizona, Trans-Mississippi Department (January-May 1864)

2nd [or Central] Sub-district of Texas, District of Texas, New Mexico, and Arizona, Trans-Mississippi Department (June-September 1864)

6th (Hébert's) Texas Division, 2nd (Hébert's) Texas Division 3rd Corps, Trans-Mississippi Department (September 1864-May 1865)

Battles: San Luis Pass [destruction of the *Columbia*] (April 5-6, 1862)

near Velasco, Texas (July 4, 1862)

Stirling's Plantation (September 29, 1863)

276. TEXAS 14TH INFANTRY REGIMENT

Organization: Organized in early 1862. Surrendered by General E. K. Smith, commanding Trans-Mississippi Department, on May 26, 1865.

First Commander: Edward Clark (Colonel)

Field Officers: William Byrd (Lieutenant Colonel)

Augustus H. Rogers (Major)

Assignments: Eastern District of Texas, Department of Texas (May 1862)

Eastern District of Texas, Trans-Mississippi Department (May-August 1862)

Randal's Brigade, McCulloch's Division, District of Arkansas, Trans-Mississippi Department (September 1862)

Randal's Brigade, McCulloch's Division, 2nd Corps, Trans-Mississippi Department (September 1862-January 1863)

Randal's Brigade, McCulloch's-Walker's Division, District of Arkansas, Trans-Mississippi Department (February-March 1863)

Randal's Brigade, Walker's Division, District of West Louisiana, Trans-Mississippi Department (May 1863-April 1864)

Randal's-Maclay's Brigade, Walker's Division, District of Arkansas, Trans-Mississippi Department (April-May 1864)

Maclay's Brigade, Walker's Division, District of West Louisiana, Trans-Mississippi Department (May-September 1864)

3rd (Maclay's) Texas Brigade, 1st (Forney's) Texas Division, 1st Corps, Trans-Mississippi Department (September 1864-May 1865)

Battles: Red River Campaign (March-May 1864)

Camden Expedition (March-May 1864)

Mansfield (April 8, 1864)

Pleasant Hill (April 9, 1864)

Jenkins' Ferry (April 30, 1864)

277.   TEXAS 15TH INFANTRY REGIMENT

Organization: Organized by the increase of the 1st Infantry Battalion to a regiment in early 1862.   Surrendered by General E. K. Smith, commanding Trans-Mississippi Department, on May 26, 1865.

First Commander: Joseph W. Speight (Colonel)

Field Officers: John W. Daniel (Major, Lieutenant Colonel)

James E. Harrison (Lieutenant Colonel, Colonel)

Assignments: Trans-Mississippi Department (May-August 1862)

Randal's Brigade, McCulloch's Division, District of Arkansas, Trans-Mississippi Department (August-September 1862)

Randal's Brigade, McCulloch's Division, 2nd Corps, Army of the West, Trans-Mississippi Department (September 1862-January 1863)

Speight's Brigade, Indian Territory (January-March 1863)

Speight's Brigade, Indian Territory, District of Arkansas, Trans-Mississippi Department (March-April 1863)

Speight's Brigade, Sub-district of Southwestern Louisiana, District of West Louisiana, Trans-Mississippi Department (September-November 1863)

4th Brigade, Walker's Division, District of West Louisiana, Trans-Mississippi Department (November 1863-April 1864)

4th Brigade, Walker's Division, District of Arkansas, Trans-Mississippi Department (April-May 1864)

4th Brigade, Walker's Division, District of West Louisiana, Trans-Mississippi Department (May-August 1864)

4th (King's) Texas Brigade, 2nd (Polignac's) Division, 1st Corps, Trans-Mississippi Department (September 1864-February 1865)

Harrison's Brigade, District of Texas, New Mexico, and Arizona, Trans-Mississippi Department (February-April 1865)

Harrison's Brigade, Maxey's Division, District of Texas, New Mexico, and Arizona, Trans-Mississippi Department (April-May 1865)

Battles: Stirling's Plantation (September 29, 1863)

Teche Campaign (October 3-November 30, 1863)

Bayou Bourbeau (November 3, 1863)

Red River Campaign (March-May 1864)

Camden Expedition (March-May 1864)

278. TEXAS 16TH INFANTRY REGIMENT

Organization: Organized ca. January 1862. Surrendered by General E. K. Smith, commanding Trans-Mississippi Department, on May 26, 1865.

First Commander: George Flournoy (Colonel)

Field Officers: William H. Redwood (Major, Lieutenant Colonel)

Xenophon B. Saunders (Major)

James E. Shepard (Lieutenant Colonel)

Assignments: Department of Texas (January-February 1862)

Eastern District of Texas, Department of Texas (February-May 1862)

Eastern District of Texas, Trans-Mississippi Department (May-August 1862)

Flournoy's Brigade, Nelson's-McCulloch's Division, 2nd Corps, Trans-Mississippi Department (September 1862-January 1863)

McCulloch's-Flournoy's Brigade, McCulloch's-Walker's Division, District of Arkansas, Trans-Mississippi Department (February-March 1863)

Flournoy's-Scurry's Brigade, Walker's Division, District of West Louisiana, Trans-Mississippi Department (May 1863-April 1864)

Scurry's-Waterhouse's Brigade, Walker's Division, District of Arkansas, Trans-Mississippi Department (April-May 1864)

Waterhouse's Brigade, Walker's Division, District of West Louisiana, Trans-Mississippi Department (May-September 1864)

2nd (Waterhouse's) Texas Brigade, 1st (Forney's) Texas Division, 1st Corps, Trans-Mississippi Department (September 1864-May 1865)

Battles: Milliken's Bend (June 7, 1863)

Red River Campaign (March-May 1864)

Camden Expedition (March-May 1864)

Mansfield (April 8, 1864)

Pleasant Hill (April 9, 1864)

Jenkins' Ferry (April 30, 1864)

279. TEXAS 17TH INFANTRY REGIMENT

Organization: Organized ca. January 1862. Surrendered by General E. K. Smith, commanding Trans-Mississippi Department, on May 26, 1865.
First Commander: Robert T. P. Allen (Colonel)
Field Officers: Robert D. Allen (Major)
George W. Jones (Lieutenant Colonel, Colonel)
Joseph Z. Miller (Major, Lieutenant Colonel)
John W. Tabor (Major)
Assignments: Department of Texas (January-February 1862)
Eastern District of Texas, Department of Texas (February-May 1862)
Eastern District of Texas, Trans-Mississippi Department (May-August 1862)
Flournoy's Brigade, Nelson's-McCulloch's Division, 2nd Corps, Trans-Mississippi Department (September 1862-January 1863)
Flournoy's Brigade, McCulloch's-Walker's Division, District of Arkansas, Trans-Mississippi Department (February-March 1863)
McCulloch's-Flournoy's-Scurry's Brigade, Walker's Division, District of West Louisiana, Trans-Mississippi Department (May 1863-April 1864)
Scurry's-Waterhouse's Brigade, Walker's Division, District of Arkansas, Trans-Mississippi Department (April-May 1864)
Waterhouse's Brigade, Walker's Division, District of West Louisiana, Trans-Mississippi Department (May-September 1864)
2nd (Waterhouse's) Texas Brigade, 1st (Forney's) Texas Division, 1st Corps, Trans-Mississippi Department (September 1864-May 1865)
Battles: Milliken's Bend (June 7, 1863)
Red River Campaign (March-May 1864)
Camden Expedition (March-May 1864)
Mansfield (April 8, 1864)
Pleasant Hill (April 9, 1864)
Jenkins' Ferry (April 30, 1864)

280. TEXAS 18TH INFANTRY REGIMENT

Organization: Organized in early 1862. Surrendered by General E. K. Smith, commanding Trans-Mississippi Department, on May 26, 1865.
First Commander: William B. Ochiltree (Colonel)
Field Officers: Thomas R. Bonner (Major, Lieutenant Colonel, Colonel)
David B. Culberson (Lieutenant Colonel, Colonel)
Matthew A. Gaston (Major)
Wilburn H. King (Major, Lieutenant Colonel, Colonel)
John R. Watson (Major, Lieutenant Colonel, Colonel)
Joseph G. W. Wood (Major, Lieutenant Colonel, Colonel)

Assignments: Eastern District of Texas, Department of Texas (February-May 1862)

Eastern District of Texas, Trans-Mississippi Department (May-August 1862)

Young's Brigade, McCulloch's Division, 2nd Corps, Trans-Mississippi Department (September 1862-January 1863)

Young's-Hawes' Brigade, McCulloch's-Walker's Division, District of Arkansas, Trans-Mississippi Department (February-March 1863)

Hawes'-Waul's Brigade, Walker's Division, District of West Louisiana, Trans-Mississippi Department (May 1863-April 1864)

Waul's Brigade, Walker's Division, District of Arkansas, Trans-Mississippi Department (April-May 1864)

Waul's Brigade, Walker's Division, District of Arkansas, Trans-Mississippi Department (May-September 1864)

1st (Waul's) Texas Brigade, 1st (Forney's) Texas Division, 1st Corps, Trans-Mississippi Department (September 1864-May 1865)

Battles: Young's Point (June 9, 1863)

Bayou Bourbeau (November 3, 1863)

Red River Campaign (March-May 1864)

Camden Expedition (March-May 1864)

Mansfield (April 8, 1864)

Pleasant Hill (April 9, 1864)

Jenkins' Ferry (April 30, 1864)

281.   TEXAS 19TH INFANTRY REGIMENT

Organization: Organized ca. May 13, 1862. Surrendered by General E. K. Smith, commanding Trans-Mississippi Department, on May 26, 1865.

First Commander: Richard Waterhouse, Jr. (Colonel)

Field Officers: Augustus C. Allen (Major)

William L. Crawford (Major, Lieutenant Colonel)

Robert H. Graham (Lieutenant Colonel)

Ennis W. Taylor (Major, Lieutenant Colonel, Colonel)

Assignments: Eastern District of Texas, Department of Texas (May 1862)

Eastern District of Texas, Trans-Mississippi Department (May-August 1862)

Flournoy's Brigade, Nelson's-McCulloch's Division, 2nd Corps, Trans-Mississippi Department (September 1862-January 1863)

Flournoy's Brigade, McCulloch's-Walker's Division, District of Arkansas, Trans-Mississippi Department (February-March 1863)

McCulloch's-Flournoy's-Scurry's Brigade, Walker's Division, District of West Louisiana, Trans-Mississippi Department (May 1863-April 1864)

Scurry's-Waterhouse's Brigade, Walker's Division, District of Arkansas, Trans-Mississippi Department (April-May 1864)

Waterhouse's Brigade, Walker's Division, District of West Louisiana, Trans-Mississippi Department (May-September 1864)

2nd (Waterhouse's) Texas Brigade, 1st (Forney's) Texas Division, 1st Corps, Trans-Mississippi Department (September 1864-May 1865)

Battles: Milliken's Bend (June 7, 1863)

Red River Campaign (March-May 1864)

Camden Expedition (March-May 1864)

Mansfield (April 8, 1864)

Pleasant Hill (April 9, 1864)

Jenkins' Ferry (April 30, 1864)

282. TEXAS 20TH INFANTRY REGIMENT

Organization: Organized in the spring of 1862. Surrendered by General E. K. Smith, commanding Trans-Mississippi Department, on May 26, 1865.

First Commander: Henry M. Elmore (Colonel)

Field Officers: Leonard A. Abercrombie (Lieutenant Colonel)

Robert E. Bell (Major)

Assignments: Eastern District of Texas, Department of Texas (May 1862)

Eastern District of Texas, Trans-Mississippi Department (May-August 1862)

District of Texas, Trans-Mississippi Department (August-December 1862)

District of Texas, New Mexico, and Arizona, Trans-Mississippi Department (December 1862-January 1863)

Eastern Sub-district, District of Texas, New Mexico, and Arizona, Trans-Mississippi Department (February-June 1863)

Debray's Brigade, Scurry's Division [or Eastern Sub-district], District of Texas, New Mexico, and Arizona, Trans-Mississippi Department (June-November 1863)

Rainey's Brigade, Eastern Sub-district, District of Texas, New Mexico, and Arizona, Trans-Mississippi Department (November-December 1863)

Rainey's Brigade, Slaughter's Division [or Eastern Sub-district], District of Texas, New Mexico, and Arizona, Trans-Mississippi Department (December 1863-March 1864)

1st [or Eastern] Sub-district, District of Texas, New Mexico, and Arizona, Trans-Mississippi Department (April-September 1864)

5th (Hawes') Texas Brigade, 2nd (Hébert's) Texas Division, 3rd Corps, Trans-Mississippi Department (September 1864-February 1865)

Harrison's Brigade, Maxey's Division, District of Texas, New Mexico, and Arizona, Trans-Mississippi Department (April-May 1865)

Battle: Galveston Island (January 1, 1863)

283. TEXAS 21ST INFANTRY BATTALION

Organization: Organized with six companies in early 1862. Consolidated with the 11th Cavalry and Infantry Battalion and designated as the 21st Infantry Regiment in November 1864.

First Commander: William H. Griffin (Major, Lieutenant Colonel)

Field Officer: H. A. Hammer (Major)

Assignments: Eastern District, Department of Texas (April-May 1862)

Trans-Mississippi Department (May-August 1862)

Eastern Sub-district, District of Texas, Trans-Mississippi Department (August-December 1862)

District of Texas, New Mexico, and Arizona, Trans-Mississippi Department (December 1862-January 1863)

Eastern Sub-district, District of Texas, New Mexico, and Arizona, Trans-Mississippi Department (February-June 1863)

Luckett's Brigade, Scurry's Division [or Eastern Sub-district], District of Texas, New Mexico, and Arizona, Trans-Mississippi Department (June-December 1863)

Rainey's Brigade, Slaughter's Division [or Eastern Sub-district], District of Texas, New Mexico, and Arizona, Trans-Mississippi Department (December 1863-January 1864)

Eastern Sub-district, District of Texas, New Mexico, and Arizona, Trans-Mississippi Department (January-September 1864)

6th (Hébert's) Texas Brigade, 2nd (Hébert's) Texas Division 3rd Corps, Trans-Mississippi Department (September-November 1864)

Battles: Galveston Island (January 1, 1863)

Sabine Pass [detachment] (April 18, 1863)

Sabine Pass [Companies D & F] (September 8, 1863)

Calcasieu Pass (May 6, 1864)

284. TEXAS 21ST INFANTRY REGIMENT

Organization: Organized by the consolidation of the 21st Infantry Battalion and the 11th Cavalry and Infantry Battalion in November 1864. Surrendered by General E. K. Smith, commanding Trans-Mississippi Department, on May 26, 1865.

First Commander: Ashley W. Spaight (Colonel)

Field Officers: William H. Griffin (Lieutenant Colonel)

Felix C. McReynolds (Major)

Assignment: 6th (Hébert's) Texas Brigade, 2nd (Hébert's) Texas Division 3rd Corps, Trans-Mississippi Department (November 1864-May 1865)

285. TEXAS 22ND INFANTRY REGIMENT

Organization: Organized by the increase of the 5th Infantry Battalion to a regiment in early 1862. Company E was captured at Fort DeRussy, Louisiana on March 14, 1864. Surrendered by General E. K. Smith, commanding Trans-Mississippi Department, on May 26, 1865.

First Commander: Richard B. Hubbard (Colonel)

Field Officers: John J. Canon (Major, Lieutenant Colonel)

Elias E. Lott (Lieutenant Colonel)

Benjamin F. Parkes (Major)

Assignments: Eastern District of Texas, Department of Texas (February-May 1862)

Trans-Mississippi Department (May-August 1862)

District of Arkansas, Trans-Mississippi Department (August-September 1862)

Young's Brigade, McCulloch's Division, 1st Corps, Trans-Mississippi Department (September 1862)

Young's Brigade, McCulloch's Division, 2nd Corps, Trans-Mississippi Department (December 1862-January 1863)

Young's-Hawes' Brigade, McCulloch's-Walker's Division, District of Arkansas, Trans-Mississippi Department (February-March 1863)

Hawes'-Waul's Brigade, Walker's Division, District of West Louisiana, Trans-Mississippi Department (May 1863-April 1864)

Waul's Brigade, Walker's Division, District of Arkansas, Trans-Mississippi Department (April-May 1864)

Waul's Brigade, Walker's Division, District of West Louisiana, Trans-Mississippi Department (May-September 1864)

1st (Waul's) Texas Brigade, 1st (Forney's) Texas Division, 1st Corps, Trans-Mississippi Department (September 1864-May 1865)

Battles: Young's Point (June 7, 1863)

Red River Campaign (March-May 1864)

Camden Expedition (March-May 1864)

Fort DeRussy [Company E] (March 14, 1864)

Mansfield (April 8, 1864)

Pleasant Hill (April 9, 1864)

Jenkins' Ferry (April 30, 1864)

Calcasieu Pass (May 6, 1864)

286. TEXAS 31ST INFANTRY BATTALION, STATE TROOPS

Organization: Organized in late 1863. Apparently failed to complete its organization.

287.   TEXAS BATES' INFANTRY BATTALION

Organization: Organized by the reduction of the 13th Infantry Regiment to a battalion ca. July 1862. Again increased to a regiment and redesignated as the 13th Infantry Regiment in early 1863.

First Commander: Joseph Bates (Lieutenant Colonel)

Field Officer: Henry P. Cayce (Major)

Assignments: Western District of Texas, Trans-Mississippi Department (July-May 1862)

District of Texas, Trans-Mississippi Department (August-December 1862)

District of Texas, New Mexico, and Arizona, Trans-Mississippi Department (December 1862-January 1863)

Eastern Sub-district, District of Texas, New Mexico, and Arizona, Trans-Mississippi Department (January-May 1863)

288.   TEXAS BUCHEL'S INFANTRY BATTALION

Organization: This unit does not appear in the *Official Records.*

First Commander: Augustus Buchel (Lieutenant Colonel)

289.   TEXAS WAUL'S LEGION INFANTRY REGIMENT

Organization: Organized with 12 companies at Brenham in early 1862. Divided into two battalions later in 1862. Regiment surrendered at Vicksburg, Warren County, Mississippi on July 4, 1863. Paroled at Vicksburg, Warren County, Mississippi in July 1863. Declared exchanged on September 12, 1863. Reorganized at Houston in the fall of 1863. Surrendered by General E. K. Smith, commanding Trans-Mississippi Department, on May 26, 1865. SEE ALSO: Texas Waul's Legion Cavalry Battalion and Texas Waul's Legion Artillery Battery.

First Commander: Thomas N. Waul (Colonel)

Field Officers: E. S. Bolling (Major)

Allen Cameron (Major)

Otto Nathusius (Major)

Oliver Steele (Major)

Barnard Timmons (Lieutenant Colonel, Colonel)

James Wrigley (Lieutenant Colonel)

Assignments: Eastern District of Texas, Trans-Mississippi Department (May-August 1862)

Waul's Legion, Lovell's Division, District of the Mississippi, Department #2 (September-October 1862)

Waul's Legion, Loring's Division, Lovell's Corps, Army of West Tennessee, Department of Mississippi and East Louisiana (October-December 1862)

Waul's Legion, Loring's Division, Lovell's Corps, Army of North Mississippi, Department of Mississippi and East Louisiana (December 1862-January 1863)

Waul's Legion, Loring's Division, Army of the Department of Mississippi and East Louisiana (January 1863)

Waul's Legion, 2nd Military District, Department of Mississippi and East Louisiana (January-March 1863)

Moore's Brigade, Loring's Division, 2nd Military District, Department of Mississippi and East Louisiana (April 1863)

Moore's Brigade, Loring's Division, Department of Mississippi and East Louisiana (April 1863)

Waul's Legion, Stevenson's Division, Department of Mississippi and East Louisiana (April-July 1863)

Luckett's Brigade, Eastern Sub-district, District of Texas, New Mexico, and Arizona, Trans-Mississippi Department (November-December 1863)

Waul's Brigade, Slaughter's Division [or Eastern Sub-district], District of Texas, New Mexico, and Arizona, Trans-Mississippi Department (December 1863)

Luckett's Brigade, Eastern Sub-district, District of Texas, New Mexico, and Arizona, Trans-Mississippi Department (December 1863-January 1864)

Eastern Sub-district, District of Texas, New Mexico, and Arizona, Trans-Mississippi Department (January-February 1864)

1st Sub-district, District of Texas, New Mexico, and Arizona, Trans-Mississippi Department (May-September 1864)

5th (Hawes') Texas Brigade, 2nd (Hébert's) Texas Division, 3rd Corps, Trans-Mississippi Department (September 1864-May 1865)

Battles: Fort Pemberton (March 11-April 5, 1863)

Vicksburg Campaign (May-July 1863)

Vicksburg Siege (May-July 1863)

BIBLIOGRAPHY

Amman, William. *Personnel of the Civil War*. 2 volumes. New York: Thomas Yoseloff, 1961. Provides valuable information on local unit designations, general officers' assignments and organizational data on geographical commands.

Boatner, Mark Mayo III. *The Civil War Dictionary*. New York: David McKay Company, 1959. Provides thumbnail sketches of leaders, battles, campaigns, events and units.

Bowman, John S. *The Civil War Almanac*. New York: Facts On File, 1982. Basically a chronology, it is valuable for its 130 biographical sketches, many of them of military personalities.

Daniel, Larry J. *Cannoneers in Gray: The Field Artillery of the Army of Tennessee, 1861–1865*. University, Alabama. University of Alabama Press, 1984. An excellent study of the artillery in the western theater.

Evans, Clement A., ed. *Confederate Military History*. 13 volumes. Atlanta: Confederate Publishing Company, 1899. Each volume of this series primarily provides the histories of one or two states. Each state military account was written by a different participant in the war, and they vary greatly in quality. All accounts, however, include biographies of the generals from their state. The lack of a comprehensive index is the major drawback of this work. Volume XI includes the Texas Chapter by Colonel O. M. Roberts.

Fitzhugh, Lester N. *Texas Batteries, Battalions, Regiments, Commanders and Field Officers, Confederate States Army 1861–1865*. Midlothian, Texas: Mirror Press, 1959. Listing of Texas units and ranking officers.

Freeman, Douglas Southall. *Lee's Lieutenants: A Study in Command*. 3 volumes. New York: Charles Scribner's Sons, 1941–1946. The premier narrative study of the organizational and command structure of the Army of Northern Virginia.

————. *R.E. Lee: A Biography*. 4 volumes. New York: Charles Scribner's Sons, 1934–1935. Also provides organizational information on the Army of Northern Virginia.

Johnson, Robert Underwood, and Buel, Clarence Clough, eds. *Battle and Leaders of the Civil War*. 4 volumes. New York: The Century Company, 1887. Reprinted 1956. Exceptionally valuable for its tables of organization for major engagements.

Krick, Robert K. *Lee's Colonels: A Biographical Register of the Field Officers of the Army of Northern Virginia*. 2nd edition. Dayton, Ohio: Press of Morningside Bookstore, 1984. Brief but very informative sketches of the 1,965 field-grade officers who at one time or another served with the Army of Northern Virginia but never achieved the the rank of brigadier general. The second edition also includes a listing by name and unit of those field-grade officers who never served with Lee.

Long, E.B. and Barbara. *The Civil War Day By Day: An Almanac 1861–1865*. Garden City, New York: Doubleday, 1971. An excellent chronology of the conflict, with much information on the organizational changes command assignments.

Lonn, Ella. *Foreigners in the Confederacy*. Chapel Hill: University of North Carolina, 1940. Accounts of the foreign-born contribution to the Confederacy.

National Archives, Record Group 109. Microfilm compilation of the service records of every known Confederate soldier, organized by unit. The caption cards and record-of-events cards at the beginning of each unit provide much valuable information on the units' organizational history.

Scharf, J. Thomas. *History of the Confederate States Navy: From Its Organization to the Surrender of Its Last Vessels*. Albany: Joseph McDonough, 1887. A rather disjointed narrative that provides some insight into operations along the Southern coast and on the inland waterways. Unfortunately, it lacks an adequate index.

Sifakis, Stewart. *Who Was Who in the Civil War*. New York: Facts On File, 1988.
――――. *Who Was Who in the Confederacy*. New York: Facts On File, 1989. Together both works include biographies of over 1,000 participants who served the South during the Civil War. The military entries include much information on regiments and higher commands.

U.S. Navy Department. *Official Records of the Union and Confederate Navies in the War of the Rebellion*. 31 volumes. Washington: Government Printing Office, 1894–1927. Provides much valuable information on the coastal and riverine operations of the Civil War.

U.S. War Department. *The War of the Rebellion: A Compilation of the Official Records of the Union and Confederate Armies*. 70 volumes in 128 books divided into four series, plus atlas. Washington: Government Printing Office, 1881–1901. While difficult to use, this set provides a gold mine of information. Organized by campaigns in specified geographic regions, the volumes are divided into postaction reports and correspondence. The information contained in the hundreds of organizational tables proved invaluable for my purposes.

Wakelyn, Jon L. *Biographical Dictionary of the Confederacy*. Westport, Conn.: Greenwood Press, 1977. Short biographies of 651 leaders of the Confederacy. However, the selection criteria among the military leaders is somewhat haphazard.

Warner Ezra J. *Generals in Gray: Lives of the Confederate Commanders*. Baton Rouge: Louisiana State University Press, 1959. Sketches of the 425 Southern generals. Good coverage of pre- and postwar careers. The wartime portion of the entries leaves something to be desired.

Wise, Jennings Cropper. *The Long Arm of Lee: The History of the Artillery of the Army of Northern Virginia*. Lynchburg, Virginia: J.P. Bell Co., 1915. Reprinted 1959. An excellent study of Lee's artillery, providing valuable information on batteries and their commanders and organizational assignments.

Wright, Marcus J. *General Officers of the Confederate Army*. New York: Neale Publishing Co., 1911. Long the definitive work on the Confederate command structure, it was superseded by Ezra J. Warner's work.

————. *Texas in the War: 1861–1865*. Hillsboro, Texas: The Hill Junior College Press, 1965. The annotations of editor Harold B. Simpson add much valuable organizational information to the original edition.

PERIODICALS

Civil War Times Illustrated, its predecessor *Civil War Times*, *American History Illustrated* and *Civil War History*. In addition, the *Southern Historical Society Papers* (47 vols., 1876–1930) are a gold mine of information on Confederate units and leaders.

TEXAS
BATTLE INDEX

References are to record numbers, not page numbers.

2nd Bull Run, Virginia 244, 255, 258

Abbeville, Mississippi 237

Allatoona, Georgia 159, 167, 190, 269

Antietam, Maryland 244, 255, 258

Appomattox Court House, Virginia 244, 255, 258

Aransas Bay 134

Arkansas Post, Arkansas 28, 169, 173, 175, 181, 182, 262, 271

Atchafalaya River, Louisiana 114, 194, 198, 234

Atlanta, Georgia 159, 167, 190, 269, 271

Atlanta Campaign, Georgia 54, 137, 151, 155, 157, 159, 161, 167, 169, 173, 175, 181, 182, 184, 190, 262, 264, 269, 271

Atlanta Siege, Georgia 54, 137, 151, 155, 157, 159, 161, 167, 169, 173, 175, 181, 182, 184, 190, 262, 264, 269, 271

Bald Hill, Georgia 175

Bayou Ala and Morgan's Ferry, Louisiana 114, 194, 198, 234

Bayou Bourbeau, Louisiana 36, 39, 118, 130, 138, 144, 148, 153, 164, 273, 277, 280

Bayou Cotile, Louisiana 153

Bentonville, North Carolina 155, 169, 173, 175, 181, 182, 262, 264, 271

Big Black River Bridge, Mississippi 248

Blair's Landing, Louisiana 176

Brashear City, Louisiana 32, 127, 144, 148, 153, 164

Brown's Mill, Georgia 137, 155

Cabin Creek, Indian Territory 38, 115, 149, 186, 187

Calcasieu Pass, Louisiana 29, 160, 211, 283, 285

Camden, Arkansas 186

Camden Expedition, Arkansas 28, 36, 44, 115, 150, 165, 171, 185, 186, 187, 252, 273, 274, 276, 277, 278, 279, 280, 281, 285

Campbellsville, Tennessee 157

Camp Robledo vs. Indians, New Mexico 126

Cañada Alamosa, New Mexico 126

Caney Bayou 114

Carolinas Campaign 155, 161, 169, 173, 175, 181, 182, 245, 262, 264, 271

Cassville, Georgia 159, 167, 190, 269

Chaffin's Farm, Virginia 244, 255, 258

Champion's Hill, Mississippi 248

Chattanooga, Tennessee 54, 169, 173, 175, 181, 182, 262, 264, 271

Chattanooga Siege, Tennessee 54, 155, 161, 169, 173, 175, 181, 182, 244, 255, 258, 262, 264, 271

TEXAS
NAME INDEX

References are to record numbers, not page numbers.